T0327727

ARCHITECTS OF
ELECTRONIC TRADING

Founded in 1807, John Wiley & Sons is the oldest independent publishing company in the United States. With offices in North America, Europe, Australia, and Asia, Wiley is globally committed to developing and marketing print and electronic products and services for our customers' professional and personal knowledge and understanding.

The Wiley Trading series features books by traders who have survived the market's ever-changing temperament and have prospered—some by reinventing systems, others by getting back to basics. Whether a novice trader, professional, or somewhere in-between, these books will provide the advice and strategies needed to prosper today and well into the future.

For a list of available titles, visit our web site at www.WileyFinance.com.

ARCHITECTS OF ELECTRONIC TRADING

Technology Leaders Who Are
Shaping Today's Financial Markets

Stephanie Hammer

WILEY

Published by John Wiley & Sons, Inc., Hoboken, New Jersey.
Published simultaneously in Canada.

For general information on our other products and services or for technical support, please contact our Customer Care Department within the United States at (800) 762–2974, outside the United States at (317) 572–3993 or fax (317) 572–4002.

Wiley publishes in a variety of print and electronic formats and by print-on-demand. Some material included with standard print versions of this book may not be included in e-books or in print-on-demand. If this book refers to media such as a CD or DVD that is not included in the version you purchased, you may download this material at booksupport.wiley.com. For more information about Wiley products, visit www.wiley.com.

Library of Congress Cataloging-in-Publication Data:

Hammer, Stephanie, 1974–
    Architects of electronic trading : technology leaders who are shaping today's financial markets / Stephanie Hammer-Krabbe.
        pages cm. — (Wiley trading series)
    Includes index.
    ISBN 978-1-118-48807-2 (cloth); ISBN 978-1-118-48810-2 (ebook);
ISBN 978-1-118-48806-5 (ebook); ISBN 978-1-118-48805-8 (ebook);
    1. Electronic trading of securities. 2. Investments—Computer network resources. I. Title.
    HG4515.95.H356 2013
    332.64'20285—dc23
                                                                2013004408

10 9 8 7 6 5 4 3 2 1

CONTENTS

This book deals with my fellow technology leaders and collects their insights on current technology trends in the capital markets. Their opinions are representative of how firms in the contemporary financial markets view technology solutions as a means to address business challenges. As a technologist with a long history in electronic capital markets, my target for this foreword is to provide perspective on technology and its market impacts to serve as a backdrop for future developments.

Taking a brief look at the history of electronic markets will provide perspective on the achievements of technology. It also helps us see where technology has yet to impact capital markets and how, if we fail to deal with issues like legacy systems, technology can cause a dangerous loss in agility that will leave the door open for new entrants.

Technology has been chiefly responsible for a transformation in the financial markets akin to what occurred in the manufacturing industry during the great Industrial Revolution. As in those days, technology is being applied to revolutionize business processes. The results are also similar to the improvements of the Industrial Revolution: better quality at reduced cost and the opening up of new business opportunities. Thus, a logical hypothesis is that information technology holds great promise for our industry going forward.

As an industry, technology has propelled our transformation from one characterized by mainly manual, human interactions toward one that is comprised of engineered processes. Increases in automation have already delivered a host of business benefits and open the door for a stream of improvements throughout the business cycle going forward. With greater automation, businesses become increasingly open to adopt what technology can deliver, in part because the integration work is reduced to a process of fine-tuning. In fact, in trading, much of the execution is already fully automated. The remaining—but very important—human work concentrates on engineering these processes. In this area, technologists and business leaders must cooperate to achieve maximum efficiencies. Technology is not of value in and of itself. It must be applied.

The impacts of technology are not limited to process improvements. Technology has enabled new business models. For example, regulators have promoted competition in markets, which fostered fragmentation, as in the case of the U.S. equity and equity derivatives markets. Certainly, parallel markets can be operated utilizing human processes, though only through technology can these separate pools of liquidity provide such closely aligned prices and deliver fills so rapidly across a number of products and marketplaces. In turn, this means technology enables market quality especially in fragmented market environments.

However, fragmentation has also caused greater concentration on the user side in equity markets. While the number of markets has increased, this higher number has not engendered a greater number of competitive market participants. This is the case because only more sophisticated ones can afford the innovative abilities and capital outlays that are required to achieve the types of technology infrastructures required to compete at the high transaction levels characteristic of today's equity markets.

In contrast, in non-fragmented markets like futures, market participants are less likely to focus solely on arbitrage. As fast followers in terms of technology adoption, they benefit to a larger degree from lower technology costs. Lower costs, in turn, lower the barriers to entry for new, highly competitive firms that operate just under the elite level. As technology costs continue to sink, more entrants will be able to afford to compete. These new sources of competition will in turn drive elite firms to discover the next technology edge. In a virtuous cycle, technology enables resourceful participants to gain unique privilege for a time, and then acts as a democratizing force within the industry.

The historical "Battle of the Bund" first demonstrated the value of technology in trading in a very public way. It was the quintessential struggle between old and new business processes. It was Deutsche Terminbörse's (DTB) fully electronic process versus the London International Financial Futures Exchange's (LIFFE) human-based one. While the support of German banks also was a key factor in the outcome, the automated trade process emerged as superior.

With DTB, trading and post trading were moved to fully integrated, electronic processes reducing human intervention to a minimum. In the heyday of the trading pits, some figures put the percentage of out trades at 5–10 percent of total daily trading volume. Statistically, larger traders were winning the disputes, which is a testament to the fact that electronic markets have introduced a more fair process. Through automation, the markets have experienced a move from subjective to objective. In listed derivatives we have achieved Straight-through-Processing (STP), which serves as a model for the rest of the industry.

Though technology has propelled our industry as well as the world at large, a word of caution: Technologies, including the ones profiled in this book, get old quickly. As in any other industry ours also requires continued technological change of its participants to stay competitive. For some these changes create uncomfortable uncertainties; others hit organizational or budgetary roadblocks, leaving them powerless to implement and/or even stay abreast of technological advancements. In fact, legacy systems from 1970s and 1980s already have the potential to cripple some market participants in that they are developing dangerous dependencies on outdated technologies. A few of the market participants are able to keep pace; others are not, and may either rely on a small number of white-labeled systems or simply fade away due to the increasing cost of complexity of their legacy inventory.

As an industry, if we fail to modernize, we cease to be maneuverable. But this, too, has a positive side. New entrants will have an advantage. In my opinion, the "next big thing" isn't there yet. We are focusing on the trees instead of keeping the forest in view. This is an open challenge and an opportunity for innovators. The next big thing will include technology; you can be sure about it. Who will invent the next revolutionary business process and render our contemporary equivalent of the steam engine obsolete? He or she will be the next visionary.

Michael Kuhn
Former Chief Information Officer, Deutsche Börse Group
January 2013

ACKNOWLEDGMENTS

My interviewees are first in line for recognition. Your insights make this book. Thank you for your participation.

Many, many kind people helped me throughout my project. I relied on friends, friends of friends, current and former colleagues, industry acquaintances, and, in some surprising cases, complete strangers for assistance, including interview suggestions, introductions, and more.

The following people deserve special recognition for their help: my Deutsche Boerse and Eurex colleagues, including Michael Kuhn, Michael Peters, Vassilis Vergotis, Stephan Reinartz, Roland Schwinn, Tim Gits, Steve Watling, Byron Baldwin, Axel Vischer, Thom Thompson, Steve Stasys, Tim Levandoski, Michael Hsih, Stefan Engels, Heiner Seidel, Deepesh Shah, Bill Rolfes, and Richard Allen. Other kind friends and industry colleagues include, in alphabetical order, Manuela Arbuckle, Ferry Boeckolt, Galen Burghardt, Professor German Creamer, Alex Gorbokon, Joseph Hosteny, Laura Hosteny, Abhishek Khandelwal, Nick Matic, Julie Menacho, Craig Mohan, Zein Rahemtulla, Todd Rich, Larry Schulman, Will Speck, Carl Stumpf, Stefan Ullrich, Tom Watson, and Jennifer Wilson. Several members of the Women in Listed Derivatives Group also utilized their networks to assist me. Thank you especially to Dorothy Friedman, Mary Irwin, Brookly McLaughlin, and Elisabeth Samuels.

Debra Englander, Jennifer MacDonald, and Tula Batanchiev, thank you for taking a chance on me. Claire New, my production editor, deserves special recognition for her unflagging efforts in ensuring a high-quality production. I greatly benefitted from her tough deadlines and eagle-eyes.

Finally, I would like to thank my husband, Thomas Krabbe, who was simultaneously my biggest critic and most energetic supporter. My daughters, Marlies, age two, and Larissa, now five months old and who was born mid-project, put up with a stressed and sometimes-sleepy mom. It was a good thing for all of us that the majority of work for the book was compressed into just four months.

ACKNOWLEDGMENTS

Stephanie Hammer is a professional marketer and freelance writer. She has 15 years of experience in the listed derivatives markets including time as a trader at a proprietary trading firm. She began her career at Eurex Exchange and also served as head of communications for the exchange in Frankfurt, Germany. Stephanie holds a bachelor's degree from Bryn Mawr College and a master's degree in international relations from the London School of Economics and Political Science. She is fluent in both Spanish and German. Stephanie lives in Chicago with her husband and two daughters.

CHAPTER 1

Meet the Architects

Agents of Change

■ A Vision and a Plan

The technology leaders featured in this book are agents of change, persuading their constituencies to adopt technology selectively to enhance business processes and advising them on how to do so. They understand the importance of enterprise class technology; they have clear visions and control the resources for their implementation.

The leaders profiled in this book are visionaries in that not only can they identify current opportunities where technology can add value, but also they are capable of imagining how future advances in technology could continue to enhance our businesses going forward. This creative capacity—the ability to couple creativity and technology—is a key attribute.

Always on the lookout for an edge, financial firms recognized early the value of technology and smart technologists. These firms have been early adopters of technology throughout the trade cycle. As markets become increasingly competitive, financial firms have become proponents of new technology—and empowered their technologists. Not surprisingly, smaller, more nimble participants have taken the lead in this process. One caveat is that some firms tend to view technology as a straight revenue play. These firms seem to hesitate to invest in IT except in areas where its implementation generates immediate revenue. The leaders featured in this book understand that spending on technology in other areas, like the back office, is often as important in terms of the strong foundation that it lays for business operations.

Throughout the conversations that generated the content for this book, interviewees stressed the importance of institutionalized, professional information technology structures and processes. While the business side has maintained a clear business plan, technology has sometimes been treated as a discretionary area. Technology is not discretionary; its integration throughout financial companies is essential in laying a foundation for success. What's more, formalized information technology structures are needed to equip companies to deal with tough challenges on the horizon. The recent financial crisis was a valuable lesson and, for many in financial technology and outside it, a catalyst for change.

■ Broad Focus

While the media has focused its attention on advances in technology that help firms achieve ultra-low latencies, this book refuses to focus solely on them. Technologies that are geared toward high-frequency trading (HFT) are covered in this book and they are an important topic. However, the reach of technology extends throughout our industry, on a macro market structure level and on a micro level within individual companies. Interviews address a variety of areas in which technology is being harnessed creatively to address a range of challenges. For instance, among other topics, they also show how technology can be applied to make markets safer with automated risk control and derive value from better data, as well as how emerging markets are utilizing mobile technologies to serve customers better.

The technologists that have been interviewed for this book hail from a variety of companies across asset classes. Some of the market segments that they represent are fully electronic and others utilize technology in different ways that vary, depending upon market structures. But at all of the companies and in all of the markets represented, technology is enhancing operations and, as an extension, business overall. This book is entitled the *Architects of Electronic Trading*, but to be more precise, the architects featured within it are utilizing technology to build infrastructures that harness technology in order to facilitate participation in all markets, regardless of the degree to which that market is traded electronically. They represent trading firms, alternative asset managers, brokers, hedge funds, vendors, and exchanges.

■ Great Communicators

Those who understand technology and can help the rest of us see its value are responsible in large part for progress. As technology extends its influence throughout our business, and our lives more generally, the role of the technologist only grows in importance. Because technology is for many of us an abstraction and our understanding of it is often superficial, the technologist who can communicate or translate between the worlds of technology and business is at a premium. The technology leaders featured in this book are highly skilled exactly in this area, and it differentiates them from their peers.

This book centers on the theme of encouraging common understanding between technologists and non-practitioners in the financial markets. For, if we better understand the trends and challenges facing our industry we may be more receptive to the technology solutions that can help us solve them. Technologists, for their part, stand to benefit from a more informed constituency.

Financial firms have understood the importance of fostering communication within their ranks. In fact, some even employ translators of sort, who are tasked with helping traders and technologists better understand each other, including helping them decode both trading and technology terms. By aiming to achieve a common vocabulary, they are helping to encourage cooperation in development.

The importance of communication extends beyond cooperative development, throughout the trading business, and has opened the door to new ways to encourage effective communication that includes, but is not limited to IT staffs. In one insightful background interview for this book with Pe-Ru Tsen, managing partner at rheform WorkplaceInnovation, a strategic business and design consultancy, who conducted extensive fieldwork and interviews in the financial industry focusing on the relationship between space, organization, communication, and technology in modern trading rooms, she stresses that the integration of technologists into the team environment can be a game changer: "It's all about communication. Trading room design is essentially about creating the most effective trading environment to enable interaction with counterparts, clients and colleagues in the market. New technologies have enabled faster and more complex ways of trading, which has ultimately shifted trading activities to more interdisciplinary and collaborative work. Savvy financial institutions can leverage their potential and performance with a sound and sustainable trading room design."

■ Other Important Character Traits

Great technologists are rare, and technology leaders are rarer still. When interviewing technologists for this book, character traits common among them were clearly visible. And some of them distinguish technology leaders from other types of leaders. Yes, leadership skills are essential. On top of those, technology leaders possess some unique attributes that seem to help them be especially effective.

For one, almost without exception, the people whom I interviewed were accessible, not surprisingly, through technology. While many of my interviews were a result of relationships and networking, I reached out without introduction to others. In my experience, CEOs rarely respond to LinkedIn pings. I was surprised when several CIOs responded to my request.

Across the board, the people featured in this book are excited about technology in a refreshing way. Most are natural optimists who believe in the promise of technology to improve processes going forward. All were excited to help teach others about our common technology challenges and novel ways to address them.

In their responses, many technology leaders discussed the importance of asking questions and the iterative process in technology projects. According to Carol Dweck, PhD, in *Mindset, the New Psychology of Success*, the ability to ask questions and learn from them is a hallmark of success. She argues that "[Leaders] are constantly trying to improve . . . and because of this, they can move forward with confidence that's grounded in facts."

■ This Book's Structure

This book is a compilation of edited interviews with technology leaders. They were asked broad questions and to minimize "tech speak" to help give a wide range of readers a readable—and hopefully enjoyable—overview of the big trends in technology and creative solutions for solving them. Given the privacy characteristic of our industry, the technologies profiled in this book are leading edge. Readers will understand that no "secret sauce" is revealed in this book.

The interview format was selected in part in homage to the great *Market Wizards* by Jack Schwager, and in part because it was a practical way to structure readable, discrete interviews on single topics. Though they fit together as an anthology, readers should feel free to jump around and read the important key points with regard to a specific topic.

Individual chapters cover key developments in technology as seen through the lens of technologists in the financial and commodity markets. I relied on my own research and helpful suggestions from both interviewees and colleagues when compiling the list of technology trends. Any omissions are my own.

CHAPTER 2

Business Challenges

Driving New Technology

Technology, while a powerful modernizing force, cannot be implemented in a vacuum. In financial and commodity markets, as in most other industries, technology becomes valuable only when applied to business issues. Thus, as a means of setting a backdrop for this book's collection of interviews on individual technologies and trends, this chapter introduces the major business issues impacting technology in the markets, as seen by technology leaders. It also highlights common themes among interviews. In subsequent chapters, leading technologists will provide their perspectives on the application of technology to meet these challenges.

Cost pressures, impending regulatory changes, low trading volumes, and infamous scandals have combined to create a dangerous crisis of confidence. But this book takes the optimistic view. In cooperation with the business side, advances in technology have the power to help the industry implement creative solutions to meet its challenges head on.

In the midst of some of the toughest market conditions of all time, as an industry we are faced with many challenges. Perhaps the single biggest challenge for the financial industry is change itself. The story of financial markets has always been about change; how well or how poorly market participants adopt or fail to do so has long been a determinant of success. However, change is now supercharged. Over time, as the pace of change of technology and within markets has quickened, companies have a harder time keeping up.

This rapid, concurrent change in financial markets and technology is putting pressure on firms in a variety of ways. But rather than view technological change as a problem, agile firms are turning to technology as a source of competitive advantage; the field programmable gate arrays (FPGAs), graphical processing units (GPUs), microwaves, and cloud computing highlighted in this book are delivering edges in speed and/or flexibility.

The current state of the economy coupled with the reputational damage incurred by the industry as a result of high-profile failures and cases of outright fraud, are either the sole cause or a major contributing factor to almost every challenge facing market participants today. Declining volumes and increased competitive pressure are forcing firms to trim costs in order to remain in business. Cost cutting affects a wide variety of business areas and, in the context of this book, the pressure to rein in spending impacts cost centers like IT disproportionally. Many of the leaders interviewed stressed the importance of a technology strategic plan to assist firms in prioritizing IT projects.

As Jerry Hanweck of Hanweck Associates relates, ironically, cost cutting also has had positive effects in the area of IT innovation. As firms look to increase efficiency, they are increasingly open to adopting advances in areas that deliver enhancements while reducing costs. For example, the application of GPUs brings order-of-magnitude performance increases for compute-intensive trading and risk management applications, and similar cost savings over conventional computing grids.

Achieving more comprehensive, proactive risk management is a shared goal throughout the industry. As it relates to this book on technology, the challenge is how a variety of market participants including exchanges, vendors, and market participants can utilize advances in technology to improve the safety of the marketplace. The proliferation of high-frequency and other trading algorithms combined with high-visibility errors are responsible for this industry-wide push for safety.

Across the board, those interviewed for this book agreed that since 2008, risk management has gained more visibility, as it should. Though always important for firms that were well governed, risk management is now universally viewed as an essential concern for all firms, and as a result greater resources are being dedicated to it. Technology risk management is becoming an increasingly important part of many firms' overall risk pictures. This inclusion is a direct result of technologists' insights on the risks not only of runaway algorithms but also those related to core IT systems.

Technology is vital in that automated risk controls can help the market quickly address problems like fat finger errors or runaway algorithms. Both Mark Gorton of Tower Research Capital and Jan-Dirk Lueders of CMT Asset Management stress in their interviews that global exchanges and trading platforms should be more proactive about the implementation of strict controls at the exchange level, in part so that a third party can ensure single firm compliance, and in part because a centrally applied check imposes a uniform latency penalty that places no one at a disadvantage.

Perhaps the most interesting observation among technology advocates is one that is shared among them: The role of humans in risk management is essential. As markets become more complex, technology can more effectively integrate myriad sources of information that impact risk. As Mark Gorton advises, we need to combine technology and human common sense.

The regulatory reforms spurred by the financial crisis of 2008 will challenge the financial services industry to design and deploy technological solutions to areas that thus far have resisted automation, in particular the over-the-counter (OTC) derivatives markets. The Dodd-Frank Act calls for virtually all standardized OTC traded derivatives to be traded electronically via "swap execution facilities," and the CFTC has estimated that setting one of them up could cost up to $4 million for a new firm to develop the distribution capabilities as well as the features and functions that mimic full-fledged electronic exchanges.[*] Thom Thompson, a business development consultant who specializes in regulatory affairs, states: "New rules under Dodd-Frank stipulate that OTC market participants transition to electronic, centrally cleared markets in order to achieve transparency. This operational readiness is taxing firms' IT infrastructures."

As far as providing flexibility for approaches to risk management, alternative connections to multiple clearinghouses, and permitting customization of instrument design, the best swaps platforms will likely emerge as serious competitors to the exchanges. As time goes on and swaps trading competes directly with futures and options trading, technological developments on the swaps side of the markets will more and more pressure traditional exchanges to innovate. In this way regulation will stimulate investment and innovation across the board.

Interviewees cited regulatory reform as having both a positive and negative impact on business and, more narrowly, in the area of IT. On the one

---

[*]http://cftc.gov/ucm/groups/public/@swaps/documents/dfsubmission/dfsubmission_051412_1659_0.pdf

hand, technology leaders view regulation as a helpful catalyst. Impending regulations force businesses to develop ways to achieve compliance. Smart businesses view regulatory reform as a new business opportunity and/or an opportunity to demonstrate industry leadership.

Technologists agreed that changing regulations will create additional burdens for IT staffs and will also add to the problem of Big Data, as market participants will be forced to store more data for compliance purposes. Some suggested that the availability of increased compliance data might in fact encourage firms to perform more detailed analysis that may lead to the generation of new investment ideas and overall better business decisions. Many cautioned that regulation would impact the markets in unforeseen ways. In a recent article, Larry Tabb, of the Tabb Group, cautions that regulators' actions to slow down markets and decrease speculation many not achieve the "perfect" markets that regulators think.[†] Almost uniformly, the technology leaders interviewed for this book viewed the uncertainty on the regulatory front as more paralyzing than specific regulations themselves.

Finally, in today's global markets, disparate regulations in the United States, Europe, and emerging markets can complicate both the adoption of new technology and the introduction of new products and solutions in new markets. One example is the case of cloud computing, where different data protection laws and security standards complicate a firm's decision to outsource.

The brisk pace of change affects not only those in the high-frequency trading (HFT) category. Rather, change in both technology and markets affects every participant. Even for firms that are not HFT, exchanges and trading platforms release software upgrades, telecommunications providers expand line capacity, and market data and other vendors introduce new functionalities. These are just a small number of examples. In today's highly interconnected financial markets, participants can be connected to hundreds of systems, which they must integrate and maintain in order to operate on a daily basis. Keeping up places serious demands on firms in terms of human and financial resources.

As both markets and technology change simultaneously, participants must focus on required upgrades as well as explore new technologies that could give them a competitive edge. How a company locates new technology is a monumental undertaking that it must address on top of daily operations.

[†] Larry Tabb. "The End Of High-Frequency Trading As We Know It?" *Advanced Trading*, November 2012, page 33.

Evaluating or even finding new technology is a challenge. Oftentimes, firms rely on word of mouth or peers' successes or failures. While firms are understandably reluctant to discuss the ways that they generate ideas for utilization of new technologies to generate profit, the general admission is that the task is complex.

Greater cooperation between technology universities and financial services is an area of exploration. Many schools partner with Wall and LaSalle Streets when it comes to quantitative analysis, but during the research for this book, a dearth of cooperation on the technology side was evident.

■ In Summary

The challenges highlighted in this chapter are common themes that emerged during the interviews conducted for this book. The intent of this recap is not to cover all of the challenges that we face as an industry. In the next chapters, we will hear how technology leaders in the financial and commodity markets view major technology trends and single technologies, and how these are helping the market address business challenges.

CHAPTER 3

Laying a Strong Foundation with Transformational Technology

13

This chapter focuses on how firms are making the transition to enterprise class technology and, in doing so, laying a strong foundation for business growth. Suhit Gupta, a consultant and expert in the field of transformational technology, explains how a comprehensive approach to technology can help businesses meet upcoming challenges. Thus, his interview is an optimal beginning for this book.

There are a variety of factors influencing firms' growing appreciation of professional class information technology, chief among which has been the financial crisis. Keeping a tight rein on IT as a cost center is important, and in today's tough market conditions even more so. Arguably, high-profile trading mistakes, securities market scandals, and the failure of several high-profile Futures Commission Merchants (FCMs) have prompted firms to reevaluate key processes, especially those that involve oversight. Partially as a result of the crisis and the introspection that it encouraged, firms of all shapes and sizes are professionalizing their

IT departments and prioritizing information technology to bring their businesses to the next level.

The nature of highly competitive and rapidly evolving financial markets has forced firms to deploy new technologies quickly to keep up. Failure to upgrade connectivity or co-locate in a data center can lead to a dangerous loss in competitiveness. Often, rapid adoption of new technology has led firms to follow a piecemeal approach. Some have implemented technology on an as-needed basis and, for them, a thorough technology roadmap has taken a back seat to immediate business concerns.

Much of the attention on innovation in capital markets technology lies in the areas of execution and risk management systems. As mission-critical systems, that focus is warranted. Yet the CIO's domain also encompasses core IT functions that are essential to daily business. A firm with enterprise class technology in place recognizes the importance of IT throughout an organization.

When a firm commits itself to achieve enterprise class technology, it not only takes a step toward operational excellence, but also introduces new levels of stability in the area of information technology. As both the importance and reach of technology continue to grow within an organization, and in markets more broadly, the relevance of stability and its role in managing technology risk only increases.

By institutionalizing their IT strategies, technology leaders are harnessing IT to achieve a broad range of goals that include, among others, cost savings, increasing levels of automation, streamlined processes, and expanded functionality as well as important reductions in latency and increases in throughput. Finally, best-in-class technology excites people and can be an important motivator. For a passionate technologist, that's an added upshot.

▪ Suhit Gupta, Technology Consultant

Suhit Gupta is a technology consultant and expert in the field of transformational technology. His specialty is helping firms achieve enterprise class technology by helping them to formulate, evaluate, and implement IT solutions, policies, and initiatives that improve the quality and effectiveness of their strategic goals and the efficiency of their business operations. Previously, he was chief technology officer at Maverick Capital, Ltd. Prior to his role at Maverick, he worked for Bridgewater Associates. Early in his career, Suhit was a program manager at Microsoft.

What does transformational technology mean in the context of financial services?

The concept of transformational technology is fundamentally the same across industries. While it also refers to new technologies that have the power to transform the way people operate on a day-to-day basis, it is commonly used to signify the transition from boutique to enterprise class IT implementation. This trend is present across a variety of economic sectors as both markets and market participants mature.

A company lays a strong foundation for growth and enhanced productivity when it transforms itself from a boutique firm that implements information technology according to current business requirements to one that follows an institutionalized process. Achieving enterprise class technology entails setting standards and following them to create consistency and predictability, which directly impacts enterprise risk management. When implementing new processes, firms must be careful not to introduce standards for standards' sake.

In capital markets, the benefits of technology are not limited to high-frequency trading (HFT). A wide spectrum of participants stands to benefit from enterprise class technology. Well-conceived technology installations lead to a variety of benefits including but not limited to greater business stability and agility of thought.

How are new technologies helping to deliver new sources of alpha?

New developments are helping technologists to optimize business processes, which in turn boost productivity. A better foundation on the IT side enables the business side to be more creative about generating alpha.

A better foundation on the IT side enables the business side to be more creative about generating alpha.

Certainly for firms that follow more latency-sensitive strategies, newer generation processors, greater density, and more computational power per watt of power spent are driving growth.

Accessibility is another area that has seen tremendous positive development. Gradual advances in technology are making great strides in promoting collaboration between users and machines. For example, virtual private

Networks (VPNs) and wireless work together seamlessly, which has made accessing systems from most locations very convenient.

How well a firm harnesses advances in accessibility can give it a competitive advantage. When its employees enjoy better access to key systems, it can help them achieve a variety of objectives. For example, seamless access to data and systems delivers increases in productivity throughout the workday and off hours. With the integration of consumer technology, accessibility also means that users are being more creative about how they work. Greater access to trade and position data means that risk managers have a better handle on enterprise risk. At the same time, increases in transparency give investors important information about their funds.

Are new technologies leveling the playing field in financial markets? Are these changes healthy for the financial markets?

It is not necessarily cutting-edge technologies that level the playing field. Rather, leading-edge technologies exert more downward influence on cost. When a technology has been available on the market for a certain period, costs tend to decline. The resulting lower technology costs reduce startup expenditures for new businesses, as they can achieve a run state faster, in a more robust way.

Whether this is good for markets is debatable. The number of new entrants that lower costs enable adds competition, legitimate or not. Unfortunately, lower barriers to entry can mean more trading mistakes.

That is one reason why transformational technology is such a valuable trend. Implementing technology in haphazard ways can get firms into trouble. On the flip side, smart utilization generates many benefits, from cost synergies to improved enterprise risk management. Well-implemented technology supports safer markets in part because systems are less prone to error.

What thresholds must new technologies surpass in order for CIOs to seriously consider adopting them?

New technologies have to pass the "ities" test in order for CIOs to consider implementing them on an enterprise wide scale. Whether or not a technology meets these attributes helps technologists judge whether they are sufficiently robust. Experimental technology has its place, certainly, but not in widespread adoption. Due diligence that includes not only the evaluation of the technology itself but also the health of a given provider's business is critical in the discovery process.

On the flip side, being a new entrant or a startup does not necessarily disadvantage a new technology provider in my estimation. After all, innovation has slowed at several larger, well-known firms. Perhaps their longevity should be a topic of more concern.

How has the consumerization of IT affected the CIO?

On the one hand, the consumerization of IT is a positive development because people are embracing computing technology like never before. For a technologist, that is exciting to see. However, workers are placing what are sometimes demands that stretch the constraints of IT staffs in terms of integration and user interfaces. Happily, however, the prioritization of IT projects is something that tends to resonate with staff. Most people recognize which projects are more important for the business.

Are the IT challenges faced by a mid-sized hedge fund significantly different from those faced by other market participants?

There are some great things about being small in number, as compared to a Goldman Sachs or Google, for example. The difference is several orders of magnitude in complexity. Our challenges in capital markets are possibly more complex, but they are definitely on a different scale. Google types are faced with the "how do we scale?" problem. Our challenge is the integration of many systems. Perhaps more appropriate gauges of complexity are how global a given financial firm is and upon how many trade inputs it relies. The issues that a small or medium-sized yet highly interconnected hedge fund faces can rival those of a larger player. The reverse is also true.

How are technologists helping to create edge?

The type or significance of the edge that one's technology staff creates varies greatly according to a number of factors, including strategy and market segment. It is easy to use HFT as a simple example because for the HFT community, the obvious answer is performance. For those that invest over a longer time horizon, the edge that technologists help generate is different and possibly less related to execution.

How effectively a technologist handles big data can represent a real and lasting edge. Those concerns entail, among others, sufficient and flexible storage and decentralized, secure access. How efficiently the business side can utilize data to generate trade ideas is an important time-to-market consideration for the implementation of new investment strategies.

One often-overlooked edge is on the enterprise side where a technologist can deliver cost synergies by growing at a sensible rate. The savvy technologist does not build for tomorrow. Instead, he or she builds for two to three years out with a view fixed on a five-year time horizon. As a result of the financial crisis, we are witnessing many examples of changing technology spend causing problems for firms' overall profitability. Responsible IT spending is an important consideration.

Is ROI a good measure of success for IT?

Yes and no. ROI is sometimes a terrible measure of the success of IT projects and related expenditures, as in the cases of security, backups, and disaster recovery. Cumulatively, they may be expensive and do not necessarily enhance users' perceptions of their technology stacks. At the same time, they are essential and ensure the stability of a business. The processes that they involve often detract from user experiences. While these processes (for example, security scans) may be bothersome, we still need to perform them for the overall health of the business.

Where is new technology having the most impact within the trade cycle?

Important advances are being made in the pre-trade area. More computing power is allowing for better assessment of trade ideas and superior quantitative research. Technology is also having a profound impact in the areas of unified communication and videoconferencing, which facilitates greater cooperation on trade ideas. Delays are verging on insignificant. The next innovation in the area, in my opinion, will revolve around integrating 3D features without the glasses. Finally, with the iPad and other tablets, users are linked to their content and context.

How does new technology cross your radar?

The most interesting way is by word of mouth. Networking is key, as is keeping abreast of new research papers from technology schools. Maintaining an ear to the ground is important in keeping current.

Job candidates are also a valuable source of useful information. They are eager and exposed to new developments by way of their curriculums. When I was a student, a manager in my school's technology department employed me to synthesize the latest developments in technology for his easy digestion.

I have gotten to be very conscious of time-cost-to-value ratio with regard to conferences and now prefer small roundtable events where the participation is limited to around 10 of my peers and we tackle shared issues.

Like many technology professionals in finance, your background is in the technology sector. How does your current role benefit?

Starting my career as a software engineer in the tech sector has been extremely beneficial. For one, software development teaches discipline and eventually leads to understanding better program management. At software companies, employees deal with fulfilling customer expectations on an ongoing basis. Those are skills that technologists that grow up in the IT ranks may not have. On top of that, I have ended up with the added perspective of what "good" looks like in an entirely different business.

I maintain personal relationships with former colleagues who are still in the tech sector, and those links are important to me both personally and professionally. Aside from the competitive intelligence aspect, the tech sector is important to us in finance for a variety of reasons, one of which is that companies like Google and Facebook have developed technologies that we use now. But another way that the tech sector continues to influence me personally is that it inspires me to think about our problems in different ways.

How long does an IT edge last these days?

An edge becomes stale extremely quickly if it is horsepower-related. It is a question of months maybe. That is why we focus on providing the best possible foundation for the business side. Facilitating investment ideas is an area where technologists can add lasting value in designing an infrastructure that facilitates agility of thought. Data management comprises an important part of that value add.

What are the risks of adopting new technologies in finance? Are they greater in the hedge fund industry given regulatory uncertainty or other factors?

Firms are well-advised to adopt the compliance perspective in IT planning, regulatory uncertainty or not. There are serious business risks if one ignores impending regulation. Data storage is already a key challenge and with enhanced regulation the industry will be forced to store even greater amounts. Quick retrieval of data points is paramount. Not only would that help regulators, but also it helps firms deliver the required information quickly. Rapid response time would mean that a) that firms could quickly show their compliance and b) they are freed up to return to the business of investing.

What do you view to be the biggest impacts of global regulatory reform on IT?

Regulatory reform has shifted the focus, at least temporarily. The industry is certainly concerned with reporting and compliance. This has added interesting infrastructure challenges for different financial organizations in different ways. The first and second order impacts of this affect nearly all areas of IT.

How are new technologies helping to increase transparency for investors?

Mobile platforms and better, faster database technology are allowing investors to get quicker access to portfolio information. Reporting in a more granular and frequent manner to investors is something that is becoming the new norm. The Madoff scandal was a huge impetus behind the move toward enhanced transparency.

What keeps you up at night? What are your major concerns at the moment (e.g., capacity, disaster recovery)?

A major advantage in having enterprise class IT is that risk control is institutionalized. It forms an integral part of daily processes. Having stable processes frees me up to dedicate my time to talent management. Technology managers think a great deal about how to achieve the best possible team. Recruiting new talent is always a concern. Helping us all to improve our game is important in ensuring that we do not get stale.

What would you list as the most important technological achievement within the financial services industry within the last several years? How has it been a game changer?

Virtualization, then mobile as number two. Virtualization has enabled a tremendous amount of economies of scale, even for small IT shops. It has also allowed for a level of standardization that was not necessarily doable without a great deal of planning and manpower. Mobility has changed the traditional application structures we were all used to, transactional methodology for users and administrators, and the overall security stack. It has also given more immediate and continual access to business data than ever before.

In your opinion, what is the next "quantum leap" in trading technology that will revolutionize our industry?

In my opinion, wireless power will be a game changer. It means complete independence for users. The changes that it implies have implications far beyond universal access. It even affects how businesses are physically structured. Think about how office furniture has been designed to accommodate outlets.

Fuel cells and quantum computing also hold promise, though not for a long while. I believe that fuel cells will be ready faster than quantum computing, though.

What lessons do you have for technologists in our industry?

As a technologist and a manager, I ask a lot of "why?" questions. Errors can serve as good learning exercises, provided that they are not careless ones. The process is highly enlightening. I encourage other technologists to do the same.

Can you discuss your biggest technology challenge and how it encouraged you to think outside the box?

Managing costs is a continual challenge for IT managers. It is actually a fun problem to solve. We are always prioritizing how we can implement the "cool things" that we want within budget constraints.

 Key Learning Points

- Achieving enterprise class technology entails setting standards and following them to create consistency and predictability, which directly impact enterprise risk management.

- A better foundation on the IT side enables the business side to be more creative about generating alpha.

- Facilitating investment ideas is an area where technologists can add lasting value in designing an infrastructure that facilitates agility of thought.

CHAPTER 4

Hardware Acceleration with FPGAs

Rapid advances in technology are forcing all firms to quickly adapt to remain competitive; high-frequency market participants are no exception. For these firms, the democratization of certain technologies has rendered them ineffective for extremely latency-sensitive strategies. Firms in this category are well aware that any speed advantage is relatively short-lived and are actively engaged in R&D to find the next source of a speed edge. In the recent past, high-frequency firms pioneered the application of hardware acceleration, which is the use of faster hardware to perform certain functions that were traditionally performed by slower software, to achieve minimum latencies. In this chapter, the focus is on hardware acceleration, which is attracting considerable attention throughout the marketplace.

The popularity of FPGAs (field programmable gate arrays), which allow programmers to develop custom hardware to solve specific problems, is on the rise across a variety of industries. Consequently, processes are speeding up. As the use of FPGAs becomes more widespread, financial firms increasingly recognize the benefits of these customizable chips. FPGA technology offers firms a cost-effective means to rapidly adjust their technology to address changing market conditions.

As in the case with graphical processing units, FPGAs offer an increase in processing power. Different from GPUs, which are available "off-the-shelf," the advantages of FPGAs rest in intelligent circuitry design. According to proponents of FPGA technology, efficient programming is the key to effective utilization of FPGAs. Finding talented technologists is challenging, and thus acts as a drag on widespread adoption. Chipmakers have responded with attempts at turnkey compilers to help companies quickly create FPGAs, but in the highly competitive financial industry the majority of these programs fall short.

High-frequency firms have been at the forefront of FPGA integration, in part because of the speed advantage that they offer. The application of FPGAs to date has been centered on feed handlers, as they offer advantages in dealing with the challenges of Big Data. As FPGA technology progresses, where they can be utilized is changing, and their benefits extend into other areas like risk management. For example, the integration of FPGAs into network switches means that automated risk controls can be carried out with negligible impact on speed.

FPGAs are not a panacea, but they are helping firms streamline computing processes and, in doing so, are delivering an edge in speed that is crucial in pre-trade decision making execution, and risk management. Smart firms are addressing technology challenges by selectively applying a combination of FPGAs, Central Processing Units (CPUs), and GPUs where each adds most value.

■ Jan-Dirk Lueders, CMT Capital Markets Trading, and Robert Walker, xCelor

Jan-Dirk Lueders is managing partner of CMT Capital Markets Trading, a proprietary trading and asset management group he co-founded in 1997 at age 26. From January 2005 through January 2006, Mr. Lueders served as a member of the Exchange Council of Eurex Deutschland. He started his career as a derivatives trader for CRT, a Chicago-based options market making firm that was later sold to NationsBank (Bank of America).

Robert Walker is chief technology officer of xCelor, a technology company that provides hardware acceleration for trading firms. Prior to joining xCelor, Robert worked at Barclays Capital in London, where he led the firm's European push into high-frequency proprietary trading and brought their in-house matching engine to European clients. Previous to Barclays, Robert worked at Merrill Lynch leading teams in equity derivatives trading technology. Earlier roles include founding and leading Barclays' algorithmic trading technology team with his brother in 2005, as well as building out technology to support high-touch and low-touch Direct Market Access (DMA).

Why are FPGAs so appealing to financial institutions?

FPGAs enable highly skilled programmers to optimize performance within a single piece of hardware. Depending on the manner in which it has been programmed, an FPGA is capable of performing certain functions in an extremely rapid and flexible manner.

The speed advantage is paramount for certain types of market participants, and in fact, they have driven R&D in the area of FPGA utilization. At CMT we have traditionally placed a great deal of emphasis on technology. Until last year, our technology investment was exclusively available for proprietary use. We spun off CMT's work in the area of FPGAs into xCelor, which provides hardware acceleration for trading firms. By spinning off this technology venture, we can benefit from economies of scale and fund further development efforts.

How has your proprietary trading heritage impacted your utilization of FPGAs?

An important component of our [CMT's] business is high-frequency arbitrage trading in the highly competitive U.S. equity markets. In this fragmented, mature market landscape, competition is cutthroat. And speed is an important determinant of success. The intelligent software edge is decaying. Competitive pressure encouraged our interest in harnessing FPGA technology.

Given our business focus, we started applying FPGA technology to market feed handlers. Currently xCelor offers market feed handlers for four major U.S. equity exchanges: NASDAQ, Arca/ex, BATS, and Direct Edge, and the CME futures exchange. The time to market for additional feed handlers is roughly 90 days.

One of our advantages is that with extensive experience on the proprietary trading side, we know that some instruments are more interesting than others from an arbitrage perspective. xCelor's clients can therefore use an FPGA-filtered data set to derive further speed advantages.

How has your technology impacted the market?

By utilizing xCelor's FPGA technology, CMT has been able to respond successfully to arbitrage opportunities. That is the real measure of its success—and its potential for other firms.

> By utilizing xCelor's FPGA technology, CMT has been able to respond successfully to arbitrage opportunities. That is the real measure of its success—and its potential for other firms.

What kind of speeds are FPGAs currently achieving?

As technology continues to advance, average message processing times for FPGAs will continue to fall. Today, based on Altera Stratix V FPGA technology, the average processing time for 10 Gbit is 300 ns and 480 ns for 1 Gbit. To use our Market Feed Handler for Arca/ex as an illustrative example, it can parse 1 Gbit of Arca/ex data in 35 seconds with spare cycles on the card. 1 Gbit of Arca/ex data translates into 15 minutes of live data. The speed advantage of FPGA-based solutions becomes clearer as we reference concrete scenarios.

When would you utilize FPGAs versus GPUs?

GPUs are well suited for computationally intensive tasks. A GPU is a better choice when one wants to perform floating-point arithmetic, for example. Conversely, FPGAs excel at simple data transformation.

At xCelor, we utilize FPGAs to speed up trade-related processes. This architecture allows one to do many things in parallel. An FPGA is able to operate on a physical electronic signal as it comes through a cable on a server. Theoretically, one can consume data as fast as it is delivered—at what is called link speed.

How do they compare with CPUs?

FPGAs are actually slower than CPUs, but they are capable of much more throughput. An FPGA can be programmed to perform many tasks in parallel. Many, many instructions can be carried out in a single clock cycle, which accounts for the speed advantage.

Why wouldn't you produce your own chip?

The customization that FPGAs offer constitutes a large part of their appeal. This is the FP (field programmable) part of FPGA—meaning that new circuitry can be configured on the chip in-situ. By contrast, printing one's own silicon is much more labor and capital intensive. Financial firms, while they may utilize large numbers of chips, are small users in the grand scheme of things.

Being active in financial markets requires a great deal of adaptability, which needs to happen at a rapid pace. It is simply not practical to commission a chipmaker to print a small run of silicon for relatively minor change to a circuit board. Thus, in this area, FPGAs are a natural fit. With an FPGA, one can quickly wipe the slate clean and re-program.

What advances in FPGAs will further propel their adoption by financial firms?

Where one can use an FPGA is changing from a physical standpoint. Previously, FPGAs were available on a network card inside a server. Now, FPGAs are being integrated into the latest network switches, which opens up new categories of applications from centralized feed handling (replacing traditional "ticker plants") to risk management to preparing a real-time feed for transmission over microwave.

How are FPGAs enhancing risk management?

The issue, more generally, is how firms address concerns about market safety without putting themselves at a competitive disadvantage. There are numerous ways to check risk, and the best are those that put the least onus on the customer. Market participants need to meet the challenge of how to achieve SEC compliance with the lowest latency penalty. The best way is the one that entails the least transformation of data.

In this area, FPGAs represent a real step forward. The latest switches that feature FPGAs embedded within them can permit users to check data as it crosses a switch—with net-zero latency penalty.

xCelor is working on an offering that helps firms achieve SEC Rule 15c3–5 compliance. The solution features checked-in hardware with hard/easy-to-borrow files, restricted list, fat-finger, and price checking against live market feed. It speaks exchange native protocols so existing code can be used with little or no modification.

What would you say to those who want to limit technological advances in the market?

Limitations on technology should not be a topic for regulatory debate. Market participants themselves are incented to follow principles of good governance and, moreover, engage in stringent quality testing of any and all technology that they employ. Though as the market has witnessed, gross negligence by market participants can occur.

For that reason, a system of checks and balances should be in place to catch the least common denominator. In our opinion, as self-regulatory organizations, the exchanges are the optimal place where those safety checks should be implemented. As the central marketplace, exchanges can implement automated risk management measures uniformly across the board and thus maintain a level playing field among market participants. In this way as well, regulators can be sure that individual market participants are not circumventing risk controls in favor of speed.

The most compelling reason to limit overregulation is that it negatively impacts market quality. If prices fail to change in a fluid way because of artificial brakes, market participants may become overexposed. That is not a problem that affects solely high-frequency trading (HFT), but also hedgers. Market participants will opt out of participation; they cannot allow themselves to be "hung" for regulatory reasons and remain in business.

Are custom FPGAs more prone to error than off-the-shelf hardware?

All modern servers contain multiple CPUs. They spin off a thread to handle concurrent execution. The lack of determinism inherent in this model can lead to the problem of race conditions. With FPGAs, one can program exact operating instructions and avoid such issues. If there is a bug, you (the owner), can fix it. You are not reliant on a provider. The caveat is that FPGAs must be programmed intelligently.

Is the search for programming talent acting as a drag on FPGA adoption?

Programming quality is paramount. It is easy to do things with FPGAs, but it is difficult to do them well, in an efficient manner. The bar is getting lower for FPGA usage and many in the industry are looking for a turnkey product that reduces implementation efforts. Today, programmers can write code in C or Java and a compiler like Impulse C will turn it into FPGA code. But programs like those lack the "brains" to orchestrate complex machinery. They lack the finesse to create optimal technology. It comes down to skill in programming. Skilled programmers think about each step and how to optimize the processing. Another piece of the puzzle is that the price of technology is falling, which is democratizing HFT tools.

What does intelligent code look like?

We take a lot of pride in our code. "Intelligent code" means putting thought into making the most of the capabilities of the FPGA chip. This requires a human being to carefully study what's needed and what the chip can do, and marry the two in the most efficient way. The code generated from a higher-level Java/C compiler won't do this at all; it will do what you tell it as simply as it can, using a small part of the chip but leaving much of the parallel FPGA capabilities to waste. Part of the problem is that C and Java, being procedural languages, are incapable of expressing the parallel possibilities of FPGA. Compilers absolutely will get better with time, but for the foreseeable future if you want to wring the most power out of your FPGA it must be coded by hand by a human being.

What's the most novel use that you've seen of an FPGA?

Now that switches with FPGA chips embedded within them are becoming available, FPGAs can add value in areas like microwave networks. Sending market data over microwave is a very difficult problem—especially if you want to send it long distances, as the bandwidth available over long haul microwave is several orders of magnitude lower than a full market data feed. In addition to bandwidth constraints, microwave is significantly less reliable than fiber transmission, with weather patterns causing interference and causing data to be lost. Reliability and determinism in high-frequency trading are critical. Logic running on an FPGA chip inside a switch can solve these problems, filtering down a full feed to only those symbols that are interesting at the remote market center, and adding in redundant updates to tackle the reliability problem.

What keeps you up at night?

Very little keeps us up on the technology side, as our systems contain integrated checks. We have decades of valuable CMT experience on what can go wrong and how to ensure that there are no repeats.

How did your FPGAs perform during the sovereign debt crisis?

Markets were indeed choppy, and we experienced volume spikes. Our FPGAs functioned perfectly because of the way we have designed them. The architecture allows us to handle data at Link Speed. This means that as long as the network can handle the volume, the FPGA card can handle the volume. Unlike a traditional CPU, an FPGA does not slow down as load increases. CPUs, by contrast, can be easily overwhelmed in instances of peak volumes.

Is it harder for firms to gain a technology edge these days? How long does such an edge last?

It is both harder and it is easier for firms to get a technology edge in today's market environment. For a firm to do-it-yourself, the capital expenditures involved in obtaining a technology edge have gone up tremendously. On the flip side, specialty technology firms such as xCelor now exist that are democratizing cutting-edge technology once the solve preserve of deep-pocketed high-frequency shops.

A good technology edge can last between a year and 18 months. Advances in FPGA technology are allowing people to combine processes on one piece of hardware. Those who quickly consolidate processes on an FPGA still will enjoy an early-adopter advantage.

What lessons do you have for technologists in our industry?

When looking at graduates leaving university, it is very important to have applied skills, but they do not necessarily need to be in finance. Specifically, candidates should try to get hands-on experience using tools that we utilize in the real world. For example, technologists should be able to use a real-world source code control system (for example, Subversion) and a programming language that we use (for example, C++, HDL, or Verilog);

he or she should be able to write code confidently. Conceptual training is important, but vocational skills are where the edge lies. Someone who has used real-life tools can hit the ground running. This is input that we have provided to several schools and we eagerly await the results.

Key Learning Points

- Being active in financial markets requires a great deal of adaptability, which needs to happen at a rapid pace. In this area, FPGAs are a natural fit.

- Advances in FPGA technology are allowing people to combine processes on one piece of hardware. Those who quickly consolidate processes on an FPGA still will enjoy an early-adopter advantage.

- Compilers will get better with time, but for the foreseeable future if you want to wring the most power out of your FPGA, it must be coded by hand by a human being.

CHAPTER 5

Gpus

Affordable Desktop Supercomputing

In this chapter, Gerald Hanweck Jr., PhD, provides his insights on how graphical processing units (GPUs) are helping firms gain a competitive advantage in terms of processing power. He is the founder of Hanweck Associates, a firm that harnesses GPU technology to provide high-performance, low-latency data and risk analytics to the financial markets.

33

GPUs are unmatched when applied to mathematical problems that involve massive amounts of parallel calculations such as Monte Carlo simulations. In an industry driven by speed, GPUs represent a tremendous jump in computing power. Nimble technologists, including those with an interest in gaming, have long been proponents of GPU technology. As a whole, the industry is starting to wake up to the potential afforded by GPUs. Somewhat surprisingly, one explanation for this shift in attitudes is not the fact that GPUs do a better job faster.

The industry has been less inclined to embrace GPU technology than one might assume. After all, dollar for dollar, they offer 10 times the processing power of traditional central processing unit (CPU) technology. The resistance can be tied to the technological challenges of porting large amounts of code into GPU languages such as CUDA, as well as behavioral factors such as entrenched IT bureaucracies.

In its early stages, the financial crisis acted as a brake on the adoption of new technology like GPUs. Now that the industry has weathered the worst of the storm, the subsequent focus on cost cutting has encouraged firms to reevaluate GPU technology. The financial crisis highlighted risk management as the Achilles' heel of the financial markets. It prompted the industry to rethink its current processes and procedures in a wide range of areas, certainly not just those focused on streamlining costs. GPUs offer significant advantages in risk management. They are a practical, readily available, and cost-effective technology that the industry can implement to help tackle complex risk calculations quickly. And speed matters during market turmoil.

■ Gerald Hanweck, Jr., PhD, Hanweck Associates

For 20 years, Gerald Hanweck, CEO and founder of Hanweck Associates, has been at the forefront of derivatives research, strategy, and technology innovation. Prior to Hanweck Associates, he spent 10 years with JPMorgan, where he served as chief equity derivatives strategist and led the bank's U.S. Fixed-Income Derivatives Strategy team. Earlier in his career, he worked as a derivatives researcher at Discount Corporation of New York Futures, and as a software developer at Microsoft.

A frequent industry speaker, Mr. Hanweck has also taught master's-level business courses at Northwestern University's Kellogg Graduate School of Management and the Graduate School of Business at the University of Chicago, in addition to dozens of seminars on financial derivatives. Mr. Hanweck holds a PhD in managerial economics and decision science from the Kellogg Graduate School of Business at Northwestern University, and an AB in mathematics from Princeton University

What is the difference between GPUs and FPGAs (field programmable gate arrays)?

GPUs and FPGAs are very different, and there is certainly room for both in financial applications. FPGAs are essentially programmable, highly customizable circuits, whereas GPUs are "off-the-shelf," predesigned, preconfigured chips, dedicated to doing certain things very well, especially tasks that involve parallel numerical processing. FPGAs are good at asynchronous integer processing, whereas GPUs excel at parallel vector floating-point arithmetic. One could certainly build a GPU on an FPGA, but that would be a very inefficient way to go. FPGAs are labor intensive; they require someone skilled in circuitry design and thus involve a longer time to market. You can buy a GPU off the shelf and plug it in. There is an ongoing philosophical battle among proponents of CPUs, FPGAs, and GPUs, when and for which application they should be used. Really, all are good technologies, and the answer is: "Use the right tool for the right job."

Can you provide us with a brief overview of GPU utilization in financial services?

GPU utilization in finance is not as widespread now as I would have hoped, though adoption of the technology is certainly picking up pace. Some of the more innovative proprietary trading firms have adopted GPUs. Every major bank and insurance company has a GPU project in the works, and some have deployed GPUs in production. Many of those involve Monte Carlo simulations for derivatives pricing or variable-annuity valuation. Still, I know of a large investment bank that requires two days to price its risk to the euro. GPUs would most certainly reduce that time to hours *and* save millions of dollars a year in computing grid costs, so it amazes me that to date this particular bank has not deployed GPUs.

The slow adoption by the financial industry contrasts sharply with other industries, like oil and gas exploration. That industry has embraced GPU technology with a vengeance. Exploration vessels now carry GPU-powered supercomputers on board to process the vast amounts of seismic data they produce without having to head back to shore.

What are the technological challenges of GPU utilization for financial firms?

Porting legacy CPU-based code, much of which was designed to run on a single processor, into massively parallel GPU languages such as CUDA is certainly a challenge; it means a lot of hands-on design and development work up front. Legacy code is one of the bigger problems facing the industry as a whole. Some in the industry are waiting for conventional CPU manufacturers to develop a magic bullet to eliminate the need to rewrite code. That is just not going to happen anytime soon.

We are seeing a convergence of GPU and CPU technology (for example, the new Phi technology from Intel, which is a manycore, x86-based

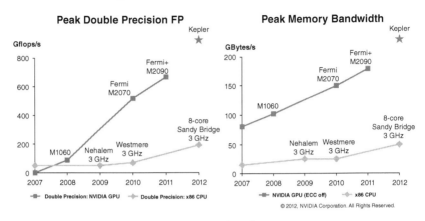

FIGURE 5.1 Reprinted with permission of Nvidia Corporation.

coprocessor). There will be a lot less distinction between CPUs and GPUs in five years' time.

The upshot is the massively parallel computing revolution is upon us. NVIDIA's newly released Kepler K20X GPU has 2,688 cores, up from 512 cores in its prior Tesla 2090 series.

(Note: Figure 5.1 from NVIDIA illustrates the growth in both GPU performance and memory bandwidth.)

Hardware manufacturers can continue to add cores at an astounding rate. But in the financial industry, software and "wetware" are not keeping pace with the hardware. Quantitative finance must start retooling its algorithms and models to utilize parallelism in a massive way or it will be at a severe disadvantage.

Quantitative finance must start retooling its algorithms and models to utilize parallelism in a massive way or it will be at a severe disadvantage.

Are there other reasons why GPUs have not been widely adopted?

There are a number of reasons that GPU adoption has met with resistance in the industry. The effects of the financial crisis cannot be underestimated when we talk about the adoption of new technologies. Financial institutions were in survival mode and new projects were put on hold. Ironically, now the resulting cost-cutting pressure is helping GPU adoption. GPUs deliver much more processing power for lower cost. But fierce resistance is still prevalent in the IT and quant development departments of many major financial institutions, where power and prestige are measured by budgets, number of servers, and programmer headcount.

What is the most novel use that you've seen for GPUs? Are there applications/uses for GPUs in other asset classes that people are missing out on?

The most unusual application that we have deployed was back in 2007 for an investment bank's proprietary trading group. We employed GPUs to filter for highly correlated groups of stocks in real time. That was innovative because it did not fit the mold of what people were using GPUs for in quant finance, especially at that time. Currently, we are applying GPUs to price derivatives and calculate portfolio risk. We also use them for more conventional data processing, such as sorting and merging large sets of data.

What inspired you to harness GPUs for financial computations/use in trading? Are you an avid gamer?

My inspiration came a long time ago when I was working at JPMorgan. A technologically inclined colleague of mine and I used to look across the trading floor and say to ourselves, "Look at all of these computers with graphics cards doing nothing but displaying e-mail and spreadsheets. What if we could harness them all to do 'real work'? How much faster could we be?" But those were the early days and, at that time, GPUs were hard to program to do general computational tasks.

Slowly, some initial crowdsourcing applications were introduced, like Folding@Home. Back in 2000 it started asking people to volunteer downtime on their PCs to form an enormous distributed supercomputer. It allows them to utilize downtime on "member" PCs to process protein-folding calculations. Then along the way some people started donating time on their cell-processor powered PlayStation 3s, and calculation speed increased dramatically. This convinced me that GPUs would be a powerful tool for general-purpose computing.

Can you describe your GPU eureka moment?

When NVIDIA released the CUDA SDK beta version early in 2007, I downloaded it and wrote my first CUDA-based GPU program: a binomial tree option pricing model. The first run was 30 times faster than my CPU! After a few more attempts, it was 50 times faster, and after a climb up the GPU learning curve and another round of optimizations, it was 100 times faster. I realized Hanweck Associates—then only three people—could build a full product suite of high-performance options analytics around GPU technology. Later that year, we launched Volera, our GPU-based, high-performance options analytics engine, as the first commercial GPU-based product for the financial industry.

Do GPUs still represent an edge?

I can answer that question from two different angles. For us as a small firm, GPUs give us an edge in that they allow us to do a lot more with less. Dollar for dollar, GPUs offer us 10 times the performance over conventional CPU-based computing grids. They are an edge in the same way that any technology represents an edge for those who know how to use it well. We have years of experience using GPUs in commercial products.

For the financial industry as a whole, GPU technology offers a tremendous edge for those who choose to adopt it. It yields order-of-magnitude performance increases for compute-intensive trading and risk management applications, and similar cost savings over conventional computing grids. Since the financial industry has been somewhat slow on the uptake, that edge still exists.

Is there a size/sweet spot in terms of project/task size for the utilization of GPUs?

The current GPU that comes from NVIDIA contains 2,688 cores on a single card. You need a computational problem big enough to require that kind of parallel processing power. Otherwise you are wasting resources. Fortunately, quantitative finance has no shortage of such problems.

Within the trade cycle, where will GPUs have the biggest impact over the next several years and how?

GPUs will have a major impact in risk management because they can help process complex risk calculations much more quickly than formerly possible.

This will allow risk managers and regulators to monitor financial risk in real time with more realistic models, without resorting to so many of the computational shortcuts prevalent before the financial crisis. Risk managers can use much more robust models of cross-asset risk, credit-counterparty risk, and correlation risk than they could in the past.

Can GPUs prevent a meltdown?

GPUs are a computational technology. They cannot prevent a financial meltdown on their own. In the latest financial crisis, many economic participants, from bank management to home-mortgage borrowers, knew the risks but chose to look the other way. The music was playing, and everyone had to keep dancing. History suggests there will be plenty more financial crises in our future, regardless of how much computing power we have at our disposal.

How has your technology impacted the market?

Our Volera technology has set a standard for what it means to do real-time, low-latency options analytics. Several leading U.S. options exchanges and major data providers utilize our technology to generate real-time implied volatilities and Greeks data for the options market. It is my hope that Volera facilitates better risk management, from the individual trader up to the board room. On a more general level, I have expended a lot of sweat equity over the past six years educating the financial industry about the power of GPUs and the trend toward massively parallel computing technology. It feels like the industry is finally awakening to the prospects.

What do view to be the biggest impacts of global regulatory reform on IT? How can GPUs help?

Dodd-Frank is certainly having an impact. It is forcing enhanced risk measurement and reporting. The introduction of swap execution facilities (SEFs) and central counterparty clearers (CCPs) for derivatives clearing is driving near-real-time risk measurement in the derivatives industry. The SEC and CFTC are striving for pre-trade portfolio risk monitoring, which for derivatives is computationally intensive. Firms have a choice. They can spend 10 times more on CPUs, or they can utilize GPUs and achieve 90 percent cost savings and still meet their new regulatory requirements.

What would you say to those who want to limit technological advances in the marketplace, (e.g., throttling speed)?

Technology is prevalent throughout the economy, not just in financial services. Any efforts to rein it in would have to be very far reaching. There is even high-frequency trading (HFT on Amazon Marketplace and eBay), where sellers use real-time, high-frequency algorithms to modify their offer prices to ensure that they appear as the number-one seller. Retail brokerage customers likely don't realize that they, too, are high-frequency traders. Orders that they place with retail brokers end up in a high-frequency, technologically intensive web of order-routing and best-execution algorithms.

On the risk-management side, high-frequency measurement and monitoring is invaluable. Regulators especially should encourage technological advances in the area of real-time, high-frequency risk management.

Is it harder these days for firms to gain a technology edge?

It is just as difficult as before. Technology keeps advancing, and early adopters have an advantage. For example, one used to be able to get a big edge from co-location or Infiniband, but now those are commoditized.

How long does an IT edge last these days?

Not as long as it used to. Advances in technology are leveling the playing field. They have driven down costs and consequently removed the size advantage previously enjoyed by larger organizations. Not too many years ago, a 10-gigabit Ethernet switch cost over $100,000. Today, it costs $10,000. A high-end 8-core server used to cost tens of thousands of dollars; now, a GPU with 500 cores can be had for $299.

Software and "wetware" also provide an edge, and the good news is that you can keep a software edge longer because it is harder to commoditize. It is still hard to program the new hardware. Ray Kurzweil predicted that within 50 years people will be overtaken by computers. Maybe, but if the current trend in software holds, I think that it will take a lot longer than that.

What keeps you up at night?

The financial industry as a whole keeps me up at night. Will the next crisis, which I believe is looming, be worse that the last one? Paradoxically, the 2008 financial crisis drove consolidation within the industry. Regulators have created more too-big-to-fail financial firms with more systemic risk and greater moral hazard. This is exactly the opposite of what regulators should be trying to achieve.

How did your GPU-based technology help your customers better manage risk during the Flash Crash and sovereign debt crisis?

Our systems were running during the financial crisis in 2008, and during episodes of market volatility like the Flash Crash of 2010. GPUs enabled our customers to keep up with the increase in volatility and data flow seen in the markets. For example, using conventional systems, it required nearly an hour for a major clearer to compute the risk of its cleared portfolios. Our Volera system now allows it to do this in seconds. A major investment bank noted that it took a weekend to calculate its risk to the euro; GPUs gets that time down to a few hours. Volera allows our trading and market-making customers to monitor their risk faster and more efficiently than ever before, pre- and post-trade.

Can you discuss your biggest challenge and how you grew from it as a firm?

The biggest challenge has definitely been running a startup in the worst financial crisis since the Great Depression. Navigating a small company through such an economy has been challenging to say the least. Being small and nimble allowed us to change tack quickly and remain competitive. An example of this is our rapid adoption and commercialization of GPU and other massively parallel-computing technology.

In your experience, in which asset class do you see technological change currently having the most impact? How quickly do others catch up?

Technology is enabling a massive change in listed equities and derivatives markets through high-frequency trading. It is changing the market structure, creating market fragmentation and intense levels of competition between trading venues. Take U.S. equity options: There are 12 listed options exchanges, which are projected to push out 14 million top-of-book quotes a second in 2013 according to OPRA (Options Price Reporting Authority). Technology enables HFT; HFT demands more technology to extract value from the higher message rates and order flow. Whether it is a vicious or virtuous cycle remains to be seen.

What would you list as the most important technological achievement within the financial services industry within the last several years? How has it been a game changer?

In the trading arena, the biggest game changer has been the commoditization of high-speed data networks, which has enabled the growth of high-frequency trading. It has dramatically driven down the cost of HFT, and thus virtually eliminated barriers to entry. On the retail banking side, developments in payments processing technology has reduced barriers to entering markets that had been dominated by big processors running antiquated, expensive point-of-sale terminals. Now one can process credit card or check payments with a mobile phone.

In your opinion, what is the next "quantum leap" in trading technology that will revolutionize our industry?

Quantum computing represents the next quantum leap. Although it is still in its infancy, the computing power quantum computing promises dwarfs that of conventional—and even GPU—computing. It will change the way the financial industry approaches everything from data encryption to risk management.

What lessons do you have for technologists in our industry?

Technologists are impatient pragmatists; we are optimistic about the possibilities that technology brings, and we want the newest technology now. Dealing with the financial industry is challenging—especially for technologists.

It can be slow moving, bureaucratic, and highly regulated. I would advise fellow technologists to persevere. There is too much money at stake for financial firms not to adopt promising new technologies.

Key Learning Points

- GPU technology yields order-of-magnitude performance increases for compute-intensive trading and risk management applications, and similar cost savings over conventional computing grids. Since the financial industry has been somewhat slow on the uptake, that edge still exists.

- GPUs will have a major impact in risk management because they can help process complex risk calculations much more quickly than formerly possible. This will allow risk managers and regulators to monitor financial risk in real time with more realistic models, without resorting to so many of the computational shortcuts prevalent before the financial crisis.

- There is an ongoing philosophical battle among proponents of CPUs, FPGAs, and GPUs regarding when and for which application they should be used. Really, all are good technologies, and the answer is: "Use the right tool for the right job."

CHAPTER 6

Microwaves in Trading

Conquering Resistance

Trading firms are enthusiastic about the speeds delivered by microwave technology. Microwave transmission of trading data offers firms decreases in round trip latencies that are impossible to replicate with traditional telecommunications fiber, for the simple reason that air offers less resistance than glass fiber. Estimates are that wireless transmissions can be up to 50 percent faster, which explains why high-frequency trading (HFT) firms are racing to adopt microwaves.

On top of less resistance, microwave technology, which includes microwaves and lesser-known millimeter waves, offers another major advantage over fiber. Whereas fiber-optic cable must adhere to terrestrial rights of way, skilled engineers can implement microwave networks in virtually a straight line (i.e., the shortest distance possible). But microwave technology has its limitations and remains a practical option for only well-capitalized practitioners of HFT, at least at present. A paucity of available channels in established markets, weather interference, capital-intensive infrastructure, and capacity constraints all present obstacles to widespread utilization of microwave transmission for trading. For firms that can overcome these roadblocks, the speed edge that microwaves provide justifies the effort.

Mike Persico of Anova Technologies, a provider of proprietary wireless networks, presents a primer on microwave technology and candidly

45

discusses its strengths and its limitations. Among other insights, he dispels myths surrounding weather effects, and shares how patented technology holds the promise to achieve availability comparable to traditional cable.

■ Mike Persico, CEO and Founder, Anova Technologies

Mike Persico is CEO and founder of Anova Technologies, a leading provider of high-speed financial and exchange telecommunications networks. At its heart an engineering company, Anova specializes in ultra-low latency networks for electronic and algorithmic trading clients. Prior to Anova, he was a part owner and partner in Ambiron, LLC, a security technology firm that focused on compliance for the financial and credit card industries. His first firm, Tekom, Inc. was formed in 1997 and has developed many of the technology standards used for screen-based trading today.

How do microwaves work?

A brief technical introduction to microwaves is helpful as background for explaining their appeal to the financial industry. Data can be very rapidly transmitted via microwaves in what is referred to as point-to-point communications. The design encompasses relaying information from radio to radio over discrete distances. The antennae, or dishes that the radios are attached to, which must be located in line of sight of each other, are serially strung together to create a contiguous network.

With microwaves, it is possible to achieve transmission speeds of up to 50 percent faster than via traditional glass fiber optics. The explanation for this massive boost in speed is rooted in physics. Air offers less resistance than glass fiber; from a technical standpoint, its index of refraction is significantly lower. The maximum speed at which data can travel is the speed of light, which is approximately 300,000 meters per second—in a vacuum. When data is sent at the speed of light through glass fiber, it slows down by roughly 100 microseconds per meter. When data is sent through the air, its speed only drops to 298,000 meters per second.

The term "microwave" is commonly used to lump together various radio frequencies (RFs) for the purposes of general discussion. The term is used as a catch-all, in a way that is similar to how people use the brand Kleenex to describe a paper tissue. In fact, the wireless spectrum includes

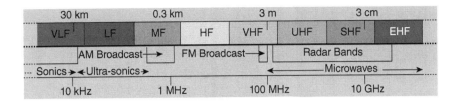

FIGURE 6.1 An Overview of the RF Spectrum

both microwave and millimeter wave technology. Microwave is actually the name for the lower frequencies in the wireless spectrum, which include 6, 11, 18, and 23 gigahertz frequencies (Figure 6.1). Millimeter waves are the higher frequencies in that spectrum. Millimeters use the 60, 70, 80 and 90 gigahertz frequencies.

Microwave technology dates from the 1950s and has essentially remained unchanged for the last 60 years, notwithstanding software improvements, as in the case of better repeaters that have helped optimize latencies. Microwave technology has remained static because of its inherent limitations, which are based on the physics of wave transmission. Millimeter wave technology, which is similar to microwave technology, has been on the market for approximately 20 years, and offers some significant advantages over microwaves, including faster transmission speeds than microwaves; greater capacity; smaller, lower-cost physical footprints; and the relatively greater availability of frequencies from the Federal Communications Commission (FCC), its counterparts like Great Britain's Office of Communications (known by the moniker OFCOM), and other such international agencies.

What's behind the newfound interest in microwave technology in financial services?

Two events have transpired to make microwave technology relevant to the financial industry. First, many people and firms have been trying to optimize fiber for the last decade, and found that process to be extremely cost inefficient and only yielded a very incremental speed advantage. Second, as market data costs rise, firms are becoming more and more selective about the quantities of data that they consume and at the same time are becoming increasingly skilled at pinpointing the subset of data that they require. Microwave technology has been both a driver and a beneficiary of this trend.

How is microwave technology being used in trading?

Firms are utilizing microwave transmissions to achieve ultra-low latency execution and transmission of key market data. Anova utilizes a combination of both microwave and millimeter wave technology to attain the highest possible availability and latency in the market today. In fact, we invented the design and process of deploying millimeter waves in financial networks back in 2010.

Millimeter wave radios are being used in trading for a variety of reasons. To begin with, they are faster than microwave radios, as they communicate from one radio to another at speeds as low as 20 nanoseconds, round trip. On top of this speed benefit, they are able to accommodate more bandwidth on their respective wave or spectral frequency. Literally, the spectrum is physically larger at 80GhZ than at 6GhZ. Most microwave networks carry around 150Mb of traffic; by contrast a millimeter wave installation can sustain up to 2Gb of data—13 times the amount of bandwidth.

Further, fiber-optic cable must adhere to terrestrial rights of way. Except in very unusual circumstances, fiber-optic cable cannot be built in a straight line, or "as the crow flies." Even if one is able to achieve a relatively straight fiber path, it cannot compete with a wireless transmission. With radio frequency (RF), skilled engineers can create a relay network in a virtual straight path, just as if one drew a straight line on a piece of paper, provided that he or she has the proper FCC registrations in place.

How widespread is the use of microwave technology in trading?

Microwaves in trading were developed for the Chicago–to–New York corridor. Chicago to New York, and London to Frankfurt are important to the trading set. Asia is just beginning the process; Latin America and Russia are clearly on the horizon.

What type of physical footprint does microwave technology require?

Because of the massive physical footprint required with microwave deployments, they are both cumbersome and costly. For example, to transmit at maximum distance in a microwave network, one would use 10-foot-diameter dishes, each weighing about 4,000 pounds. Now, this works in the corn fields of the American breadbasket, but with these mammoth specifications, microwave dishes are difficult to implement in metropolitan areas. Like all RF systems built for the trading community, each dish must be within a clear line of sight view of another, free of buildings, trees, and the like. Because of this need for unobstructed communication, dishes are commonly located on the tops of very tall buildings or as high as 450 feet in the air on towers, with the latter being difficult to find in densely populated areas due to aesthetic objections. However, the biggest benefit of a microwave transmission is its ability to achieve great distances between antenna and radios pairs, or links. It is common to see 40 miles/64 kilometers of link distance, which means that out of all the technologies available today, you need the least amount of microwave equipment to construct a long-haul network like from Chicago to New York. While that still may be prohibitively expensive for most firms, less equipment means fewer towers, which both then transpire to mean less overall cost.

In comparison to the infrastructure requirements of microwaves, the footprint for a millimeter wave transmission is much smaller. Millimeter waves require only a 2-foot dish, weighing only 80 pounds. However, millimeter waves cannot travel nearly as far as microwaves. They can travel a maximum of 10–15 kilometers. For this reason, a millimeter wave network requires many more dishes and links to do the job, and thus over long distances can cost more than a microwave network to build. However, the extra capacity and lower latency can often justify the extra cost.

Are microwaves a backup for fiber?

Quite the contrary; microwaves are being used as a primary means of transmission for high-frequency trading firms.

So, microwave technologies are more reliable than commonly assumed?

Microwaves can be quite reliable, depending on the design, but certainly less than traditional fiber or cellular networks. Wireless carriers (for example, cell phone network providers) follow a star topology to ensure very high availability. They need 99.999 percent uptime. Yet because of the point-to-point serial design that all financial RF networks employ, the availability of microwaves is currently and understandably less than that. You'll see different numbers, but microwave technology offers an approximate availability of 95–97 percent when used alone. Firms are willing to accept this reduced availability in exchange for the considerable speed advantage. And when fiber-optic networks and our microwave networks are both operational, our microwave network beats fiber-optic cable every time by a large margin. This gives firms the queue position or the rapid transference of market data that they seek.

Of course, as with any legacy over-the-air technology, microwaves and millimeter waves are both affected by inclement weather. Snow and fog interfere with microwave transmission because they create temperature inversion effects. However, rain poses less of a problem for microwaves because rain is a constant temperature gradient. On the other hand, millimeter waves dislike rain, because the typical size of a raindrop is almost a millimeter, which then disrupts the contiguous wave. One could utilize both technologies in a failover scenario, but the bandwidth disparity between the two spectrums would make this difficult at best.

Are capacity concerns affecting the adoption of microwaves?

Perhaps the biggest problem with microwaves for the financial industry is one of bandwidth. As stated before, microwaves can only accommodate limited bandwidth: 150 megabytes on a single channel. One can combine several channels to expand bandwidth, but availability makes that very difficult to do from a practical standpoint. Further, one needs available spectrum to do just such a muxing. And on the long haul, that is unlikely to happen because of the scarceness of available registrations and prior communication notices (PCNs), as well as the fact that anyone wishing to aggregate spectral channels must petition the FCC. That approval process likely would be complicated by a flood of responses from vested interests as to why the FCC should not grant permission for channel consolidation. But, firms are cognizant of these limitations when they decide to adopt microwaves.

How is the bandwidth of microwave transmission affecting data consumption?

Trading firms have learned how to do more with less. This is the result of a combination of factors, including the rising costs of market data and limited bandwidth, discussed previously. In essence, firms are no longer subscribing to the entire feed and are developing ways to strip down data to react to data signals. In a sense, we are reversing the trend of Big Data. The objective becomes how to achieve the maximum speeds with a small amount of data. We are going forward because we make things faster, but we are going backward because we are offering less bandwidth than ever before.

And as firms become smarter consumers of data, exchanges and other vendors will be forced to alter their offerings or will introduce more flexible data packages. Quite simply, the largest market participants will dictate and drive this process to completion.

How is the licensing of radio frequencies driving the development of microwaves?

There are only a set number of interesting microwave spectrums or PCNs available, and the Federal Communications Commission allocates those. And what defines interesting is the shortest line between two major destinations, like Chicago and New York. Once this best path line has been taken, you have to take an alternate, less direct (so thereby slower) route. For this reason, PCNs are in great demand; there is a mad dash going on for spectral assets in every major financial corridor in the world. People will use these for legitimate network build-out or for less-savory purposes of blocking others from having a contiguous network. The scarcity has even led to gray market, speculative trading of PCN assets. On the millimeter side, there is a light licensing process, whereby users can register their own links, but there has been the same run on the shortest, "as the crow flies" paths, as with microwave spectrum. In the millimeter wave space, Anova holds 4,000 plus FCC registrations, hundreds on the microwave side. If you look at both spectrums, we are the single largest holder of registrations and licenses in the United States.

The number of microwave channels is fixed and limited by the laws of physics. Given the fixed supply and high demand, they are at a premium. Further factors negatively impact supply as well. The entire range of frequencies in the 90GhZ range is reserved for military communications in the United States. And the entire 60GhZ range is unlicensed, making it available to anyone without a reservation, but subject to interference, which renders it useless for trading. Those restrictions leave the 70GhZ to 80GhZ ranges for our purposes.

What's next in microwaves?

We feel strongly that the integration of free space optics with millimeter waves will put wireless transmissions on par with fiber-optic cable in terms of availability—and continue to surpass it in terms of speed. Free space optics entails the use of lasers to transmit data in free space, or air. Anova and its joint venture partner, which owns over 30 patents on this technology, commercialized this out of a decade-long project for the U.S. Department of Defense (DOD). We intend to deploy this technology both in the metro area and over the long haul to optimize the entire route from Chicago to New York. This is highly notable as it is the first new technology to be developed in the RF space in decades. The real benefit here is that this equipment, by virtue of its interwoven signals, will increase the current availability of wireless networks from 95 percent to 99.99 percent.

The integration of free space optics with millimeter waves will put wireless transmissions on par with fiber-optic cable in terms of availability—and continue to surpass it in terms of speed.

Some extremely well-capitalized firms that prefer to remain under the radar are also working in this area. Their achievements are well-guarded and proprietary in nature. Anova is a vendor of high-speed connectivity, and thus our work in this area is public. We are an engineering company and we challenged ourselves to solve for the biggest technical problem with wireless: Can we solve for weather to engineer "five nine" 99.999 percent availability?

While the latency is on par with any legacy millimeter wave system, a hybrid free space optics/millimeter wave (FSO/MMW) faces scintillation as its chief challenge. Scintillation is an atmospheric condition whereby a fluctuation in electromagnetic waves interferes with the laser transmission of data.

The beauty of all of this is that scintillation and rain cannot happen at the same time. So in effect, this system will be largely impervious to all inclement weather events. This is a turning point in the history of RF networks for the financial industry and one that will make our hybrid equipment the de facto standard.

The Department of Defense is estimated to have spent 200 million dollars in developing the technology, and we have jointly invested many tens of millions in its commercialization. Originally, the DOD project was developed for keeping fighter jets in communication with each other. A key part of the design was to be able to accommodate for the jets' continually changing locations. Putting our equipment on a tower is certainly not like adjusting for mach1 positional changes, but another compelling aspect that is in direct lineage to the fighter jet product is its ability to stay auto-aligned in the twist and sway generated by very high winds.

When this technology is successfully introduced to the market it will provide a compelling argument for many firms, both within the financial sector and outside, to make the switch from fiber, microwave, and millimeter wave. In fact, all legacy RF networks and designs should be rendered moot. Additionally, our technology features the same, and in some configurations more, bandwidth as millimeter wave, with an availability extremely close to fiber.

Is the speed advantage that microwaves offers tantamount to a net tax on HFT participants?

With fiber, there are perpetual incremental advantages that cost everyone money. With our wireless offering, we seek to build the endgame—the fastest, shortest path, such that there is no need to improve. The speed of light is a constant, so if you can spectrally reserve the shortest route, you are done with optimization for good. The real challenge here is time to market. If we can bring these networks live sooner rather than later, companies can get value out of them. Otherwise, it becomes a tax on the whole industry. We're a bit different in that we are sensitive to the ecosystem of electronic trading. There is no way for us to profit if our clients do not. Therefore we have a recurring theme that we strive for: first in speed, first to market.

Are there any significant differentiating factors between vendors of broadband microwave networks?

The main differentiator is the amount of value one provides. What can you do that industry cannot do itself? Do you offer an alternative hardware? Do you offer different technology? Do you have unique spectral assets? Most telecommunications network vendors seek to buy off-the-shelf equipment and re-package, calling it "their network." In reality, there is absolutely no value to the end user there, as that's the quintessential definition of a commoditized service. What these people are thinking is that there is a lot of money involved in offering microwave technology for financial services.

This, thereby, is causing new vendors without experience in financial services connectivity and with no intent to remain for the long haul to crop up almost daily for their piece of the pie. That's not how business is done, and that's not how we operate. In five years [or] in a decade, the market will have separated the carpet baggers from the firms that are looking at the long-term, big picture.

Are broadband microwave networks ideally suited for emerging markets?

It is much easier to erect a microwave dish on the top of a building than it is to acquire terrestrial rights of way. This is especially true in emerging markets, where companies may not be familiar with local restrictions, governmental agencies, and so forth, in order to facilitate a traditional fiber build. On the downside, in those same emerging markets, you may run into a scenario where spectral assets are all unlicensed. And this could lead to a "wild, wild West" situation whereby people are setting up networks with no governmental coordination and ultimately interfering with one another. A fixed system to track, allocate, and disseminate spectral assets is clearly the best mechanism to ensure all market participants have the ability to run their networks.

What would you say to those who want to limit technological advances in the marketplace (e.g., throttling speed)?

We are of the opinion that, by and large, software flaws have caused the recent crashes. The issues have originated at the application layer; none of them are due to the physical layer or the bandwidth that resides on these low latency networks. As such, perhaps the solution is the need for a Sarbanes-Oxley type of regulation for software—something along the lines of an industry-wide, mandatory quality assurance check at the software level. It should be administered by a neutral third party to ensure compliance, to discourage people from cutting corners.

Is it harder these days for firms to gain a technology edge?

Yes, it is markedly more difficult for firms to gain a technology edge. The costs for incremental reductions in latency are rising. It costs more and more to achieve smaller reductions, and then it becomes a question of returns: Can a company benefit from the latency advantage a firm like ours might provide? The answer varies from firm to firm. We do know that many trading firms are granular and sophisticated enough to utilize a several-microsecond latency advantage. This tells us that the race to zero is still alive and well, which then bodes very well for companies like Anova.

Also, the gap between the fastest player and the second-faster player has shrunk considerably. Similarly, the gap between the fastest and 10th-fastest has also gotten smaller. The field has condensed. Low latency has become realistic for a greater number of market participants. And Anova is partially responsible for this development; our goal is to create the best-in-breed and then distribute those networks to as many market participants as possible.

How long does an IT edge last these days?

Both technological transformation and change in the markets are occurring rapidly and simultaneously. For a trading firm, the reason to write an algo—to participate in a certain asset class—is to gain an edge—to glean or extract some alpha from the markets. And the duration of the edge or alpha varies according to a number of factors including the quality of the edge and whether it software-, hardware-, or network-related. It has been lamented by some firms that many algorithms today have a shelf life of two, perhaps three, weeks. The retooling that is then required means there is a great deal of reinvestment at the application layer and in development cycles. On the other hand, a pure, network speed advantage may last between three and six months. What must be contemplated is the concept of return on investment (ROI); specifically, if an edge is so short-lived, then it must be sufficiently large enough to warrant an investment that carries a 12-, 24-, or even 36-month term. From our perspective, the challenge is one of capacity. On the fastest paths, there is only room for less than a handful of customers. And how is that bandwidth allocated? First come, first serve? To the highest bidder? We've operated through the former model, but the real solution lies in squeezing more bandwidth onto existing routes, thereby increasing the fastest path distribution to a wider audience.

What keeps you up at night?

Execution of our technical strategy and time to market are my chief concerns. With our hybrid FSO/millimeter wave technology, we truly feel we have lightning in a bottle. And there is a group of people willing to pay for a best-of-breed connectivity premium, *if* I can bring it to market where they can achieve a return on its cost to them. And if I can't, it simply is a net tax to the industry as a whole, which people are not terribly excited about. Further, if I cannot achieve rapid deployment and implementation, RF as a technology on the whole will become commoditized, similar to what is happening to low-latency fiber today.

In your experience, in which asset class do you see technological change currently having the most impact? How quickly do others catch up?

Given the nature of high-frequency firms, which largely comprise Anova's customer base, we are witnessing technological change equally across all asset classes. However, we do believe that the overall rate of adoption for RF as a product set would dramatically rise if U.S. equities' volumes were to pick up. Volume and volatility ultimately drive trading firm profits, and with more profits comes a higher spend on technology.

What would you list as the most important technological achievement within the financial services industry within the last several years? How has it been a game changer?

Exchange connectivity over a wireless transmission medium has delivered massive increases in transport speeds. And we are still at the very cusp of this trend. Specifically, every financial industry connection that currently runs over fiber could and will be connected by wireless in the mid-term. That's the United States, the UK, Europe, and even emerging markets like Russia and Latin America. Our history was forged in providing low-latency fiber networks for trading, but we are making the transition to overlay wireless onto our entire global network footprint because we feel so strongly about this new technology. We have practiced the art of self-disruption, which for technologists especially is a necessary periodic exercise. We would even go so far as to say that self-disruption is tantamount to self-preservation. From a 50,000-foot view, our current fiber build projections are relatively flat, but conversely, we see a market whereby a billion dollars in new wireless networks will be created over the next decade.

In your opinion, what is the next "quantum leap" in trading technology that will revolutionize our industry?

We will see the next leap forward when wireless transmissions are able to cross the Atlantic and, soon thereafter, the Pacific Oceans. That reduction in transoceanic fiber latency will be on an order of magnitude never before experienced. We are talking reductions in 20 to 30 *milliseconds*. This, in a trading firm time continuum, is the equivalent of literally *days* of an advantage. There are ways that exist even today to achieve these sorts of gains, but there are significant implementation challenges and, more importantly, massively high costs. This kind of research work is development without a net since it will be hard to convince naysayers before an actual network is up and running. You are putting a lot at stake and building something where you hope they will come.

And really the downtrodden volumes landscape and overall economic climate has put an end to the time when customers would pay for a spec network, so firms like mine must think long and hard about a "field of dreams" type of build. This, however, is not science fiction; we prefer the term science *faction*. The move from terrestrial-only RF connectivity to an unlimited deployment scope over land and sea will be accomplished in our lifetime. I would hazard a guess that it will get done in the next decade.

What lessons do you have for technologists in our industry?

Practice the art of self-disruption so that you do not become stale. You want to be "Your Company 2.0," and not have the latest, more agile competitor *du jour* come along and take that mantle from you. Also, build for the long term; don't build to make a dollar today. Sacrifice short-term profits for long-term market share. And perhaps most importantly, understand the concept that the field does not lie. Take what you have done in engineering, on paper, and put in into practice and into production. Sometimes in the lab, the engineering and physics look great, but in the end, the field may expose some practical flaws. Too many firms live in a theoretical world and have no deployment expertise.

Key Learning Points

■ Firms are utilizing microwave transmissions to achieve ultra-low latency execution and transmission of key market data.

■ Perhaps the biggest problem with microwaves for the financial industry is one of bandwidth. So, trading firms have learned how to do more with less. In essence, firms are no longer subscribing to the entire feed and are developing ways to strip down data to react to data signals.

■ Free space optics, which entails the use of lasers to transmit data in free space, or air, is highly notable as it is the first new technology to be developed in the RF space in decades. The real benefit is that this equipment, by virtue of its interwoven signals, promises to increase the current availability of wireless networks from 95 percent to 99.99 percent.

MICROWAVES IN TRADING

CHAPTER 7

Cloud Computing

Moving toward Acceptance

Competitive pressure in the industry is forcing firms to investigate ways to optimize their IT infrastructures and at the same time maximize cost efficiencies. Cloud computing, which includes the decentralized delivery of hardware and/or software as a service via a network, is one answer. It offers significant advantages for participants in the financial markets, which are not limited to shared economics. The agility that is characteristic of cloud technology makes it a natural fit for the dynamic financial industry. In this chapter, Ken Barnes of Options IT, a specialist provider of private financial cloud services, discusses the headwinds facing cloud computing and the prospects for its widespread adoption.

If cloud computing holds such promise, why has the industry been slow to embrace it? Among other reasons, fears about availability and security have dampened enthusiasm for cloud computing. The good news is that advances in technologies that enhance cloud computing are helping to dispel concerns. Cloud computing success stories in non-financial sectors of the economy have encouraged the financial industry to sit up and take notice; Amazon and Facebook have proven the viability of cloud computing in a very public way.

Just what is cloud computing? Generally speaking, it utilizes economies of scale to reduce computing costs for a shared network of users; the cloud moniker is traceable to the diagram used in network diagrams. But pinning down exactly what cloud computing includes has been a challenge in that the term "cloud computing" can be applied very broadly to include

59

programs like Citrix or Salesforce. In some ways, the difficulty of concisely defining cloud computing has acted as a negative drag upon its adoption. If IT departments cannot agree on what it means, how can they agree on how and where to implement it?

The centralized storage and decentralized delivery of software applications are not the center of the debate on cloud computing in financial services. Instead, its controversial aspects are associated with so-called "infrastructure as service," or in the case of financial services, outsourcing of all or some aspects of the trade cycle to a third-party provider.

Given its highly proprietary nature, the financial services industry may never fully outsource the entire trade cycle; execution may well remain in house. However, the flexible nature of cloud computing means that it lends itself well to partial outsourcing. Batch-type processing and storage are highly amenable to cloud technology.

Another area of promise for the cloud lies in purpose-built applications that can be shared throughout the industry (for example, uniform regulatory and compliance systems). Such cooperative projects benefit from economies of scale and are ideally suited for widespread, networked distribution.

■ Ken Barnes, Options IT

Ken Barnes is the global head corporate development for Options IT, an industry pioneer and among the first to host its hedge fund and broker dealer customers in a "private financial cloud" in 2007. The Options IT cloud now spans 22 data centers across the Americas, Europe, and Asia. Prior to joining Options IT, Ken was the senior vice president in charge of the platform services business for NYSE Euronext, inclusive of cloud computing, transactions, and market data integration and services, as well as the company's application ecosystem development strategy.

After having spent a dozen years in business development, product marketing, and trading facilitation roles at Salomon Brothers, Reuters, and NextSet Software, Mr. Barnes joined Wombat in 2005. As head of business and planning, he helped the company quintuple revenue in two years and launched the company's high-performance middleware products, positioning it for acquisition by NYSE in 2008. Most significantly, Mr. Barnes oversaw the company's Secure Financial Transaction Infrastructure® (SFTI) and colocation business in the United States, and launched the U.S. Liquidity Center in Mahwah, New Jersey.

Mr. Barnes earned a bachelor's degree in international marketing from the University of Vermont, attended the University of Grenoble, France, and holds an MBA from New York University's Stern School of Business.

How is cloud computing already impacting our industry?

The underlying concepts of multi-tenant hosted managed service have been around our industry for decades in the form of decision support, trend management, and portfolio pricing systems from vendors like Bloomberg, Factset, and Reuters. However, in the past the industry was still dominated by a vertically integrated IT delivery structure that built empires of complexity within the walls of each firm.

As time evolved that complexity grew. And where once it could be managed effectively by a small IT team that knew enough about the systems involved to get by, the depth of complexity within each layer of the IT stack—from networks to servers to datacenter technologies to databases to the applications themselves—has grown beyond the boundaries of what any individual or small team can handle today. The modern capital markets institution requires a team of experts, Linux experts, Windows engineers, database administrators, network engineers, security experts, support desk staff, market data experts, FIX order routing experts, and others, to work in concert to properly maintain operations. Moreover, each role must be staffed to withstand the impact of common vacations and staff turnover. Cloud, beyond anything else, is about leveraging the scale economics of a unified and complete IT team within a service provider to deliver all these capabilities in an affordable and scalable package.

CLOUD COMPUTING

Cloud, beyond anything else, is about leveraging the scale economics of a unified and complete IT team within a service provider to deliver all these capabilities in an affordable and scalable package.

It is also worth noting that gradual, but steadily rising levels of industry acceptance are driving cloud adoption. Cloud poster children such as Salesforce.com and Amazon have raised visibility and forced business to reconsider their assumptions about what can be accomplished securely in the cloud, slowly bending biases over time.

How is cloud computing helping financial market participants meet IT business challenges?

Properly implemented, a cloud solution can more closely align infrastructure expenses with revenues, reduce time to deployment of additional capacity, and reduce the cost of IT operations. These are coupled with the necessary expertise that a firm today requires to properly maintain each element of its infrastructure platform with a level of reliability and resiliency that would normally be unaffordable for anyone but the largest of institutions.

Cloud computing is providing a lubricant to the reordering of roles within the sector. Look at the trends. Regulatory changes will impose risk limits and raise the cost of capital, which is removing liquidity from the market. Firms are struggling to fund the operations of trade processing infrastructures that were built for volume levels that no one expects to see return for the foreseeable future. Increasing levels of sophistication in IT automation stacks allow for more scalable and functional technology platforms than ever possible before. A vibrant service-provider community is evolving to meet these challenges head on.

In cases like Options IT, the firm has 10 solid years of operational experience that it can bring to bear on providing large-scale technology platforms. That is equivalent to the time during which Apple has built the foundations of the company it is today, shipping OS X and iTunes. That sort of accumulation of operating experience and iterative evolution of the operating platform are what is essential to industry transformation. We are now seeing its impact through accelerating cloud adoption.

Cloud permits our industry to exit what is tantamount to IT manufacturing step by step. Cloud permits users to tap into the economies of scale that were previously only available to the Foxconns [in size and sophistication] of our industry, which are able to produce these platforms at scale.

What is arguably the single greatest value add of cloud computing?

Cloud computing offers a competitive advantage in two forms: It allows users to adjust business priorities in IT much more tightly, and it offers instantaneous off-the-shelf implementation. The cloud gives users the ability to consume data center infrastructure on demand. Firms tend to build data centers for the needs of a point in time, a projection some years away, in line with the way their firm approaches their financial and operational planning.

The problem with such fixed investments is they are properly sized for a single moment in time (e.g., the time when supply equals demand). And every day before that and after it is one where the firm is imbalanced, carrying more overhead than required or lacking necessary capacity to run the business. The desire to move beyond the constraints of these fixed investments is universal across all businesses, and the true promise of the cloud lies in offering an alternative to the traditional fixed investment model for IT.

Is adopting cloud computing a necessity for financial services firms?

Cloud is no more necessary than proper business planning or an effective marketing strategy is. These are tools that smart businesses can use to improve the fortunes of their organizations. Nor is adoption a binary "all in" decision. Cloud adoption can and should be approached in a thoughtful workload-by-workload analysis process whereby each application supporting the business is modeled based on its security constraints, functional requirements, and the financial impact of maintaining as an enterprise deployment versus moving into a cloud computing delivery model of some form.

Regulation is another significant factor impeding the widespread adoption of cloud computing by the financial industry; in fact it can be a paralyzing one. Regulations are challenging in that they are multinationally diverse, are subject to interpretation, and tend to change over time in unpredictable ways. For an executive responsible for operating a firm's technology in proper compliance with these rules, this makes for an onerous and stressful decision-making process. Technology managers must address questions like "How can I remain in compliance today, and will I still be in compliance tomorrow?" and "Which approach will allow me to do so across each of the countries in which I operate?"

Also keep in mind the numerous dimensions of regulatory oversight that must be considered. Protection of data security is the most obvious and certainly a critical one. Retention is another. Many regulations such as SEC rule 17a-4 in the United States demand the proper retention of uneditable records for a period of years. Less obvious is the issue of administrative controls, wherein staff is granted access to the rights of various systems. Many regulatory regimes are particularly sensitive to this issue and have enforced strict guidelines governing the enforcement of "least privileged access" rights. These restrictions aim to ensure that each member of staff is given no more access to and control over each aspect of a system than is absolutely necessary to perform his or her duties.

Are there customer types that are at the forefront of cloud utilization?

Adoption tends to be driven by a few key factors such as unit autonomy, the degree of legacy burdens, and of course the appetite for technological risk versus reward. Unit autonomy indicates the degree to which a given unit (a company or a department) can make its own decisions without the need for further approvals. Bureaucracy within larger firms is an obvious source of drag on would-be adopters. Legacy systems serve as another brake, as those in a greenfield situation (e.g., a startup firm) need not worry about issues such as the integration with and evolution of existing systems. Finally, technological adoption is always a subjective matter influenced by the degree to which the principals driving the decision are inclined toward the benefits of early adoption versus the relative certainty of staying with proven and well-understood systems. Examples of adoption are visible on the Street, but more often they are occurring in smaller firms and in the more aggressive, autonomous departments within the larger institutions.

Will cloud computing remain attractive primarily for non-latency-sensitive participants?

Latency sensitivity calls for the minimization of layers and removal of bottlenecks in a given system. If one considers cloud implementations that are heavy on virtualization and shared resources, this poses a real problem. A more liberal implementation of cloud computing, however, will focus on the leveraging of shared resources, which have little to no impact on performance. An example of this is a trading platform that shares common network connections and storage but with wholly independent, non-virtualized compute nodes. Clouds can be used to support quantitative trading and similar performance-intensive workloads, and are in production around the world today. Despite their existence, there is no question that less latency-sensitive applications are more suitable for a more fully virtualized platform, and therefore those are the ones being more aggressively migrated to clouds.

What are the behavioral challenges of cloud adoption from a global standpoint?

Reducing the latency of virtualized environments is a major challenge that cloud providers need to meet. On shared servers, users deal with the reality of a shared environment: You may not be first in line. The horror scenario is that you are not in control of a given central processing unit (CPU) when you need it because it has been already allocated to another user. One way to get around this problem is by exposing more controls that allow users to specify affinity, or instructions that specify "control of this CPU will not be ceded to any other application."

Within larger firms, convincing the various business units to agree to adopt cloud computing is a challenge. To start with, everyone has his or her own idea of what constitutes a cloud. However, in the current economic environment, firms are looking to save costs and implement standardization, and in those areas cloud computing has a lot to offer.

Will a virtual environment ever be the same as a proprietary one? No, but the differences will be reduced to the point where it becomes insignificant. The more cloud acceptance grows, the more R&D will be conducted and then the results will be passed on to customers. It is a virtuous circle. As cloud computing advances, it will be increasingly difficult to justify going it alone from the standpoint of both cost and functionality.

What are the technological challenges associated with utilizing cloud computing for financial market participants?

The nuances of multicast in the market data space represent a technological challenge. Other significant ones are performance in a shared environment and security. The positive news is that in all of these areas technology is continually advancing.

User expectations in those areas are changing dramatically as well. In the case of security, in the past, everyone's definition of network security was a firewall. A promising example of how technology is innovating to enhance security is a startup called Bromium. The company's desktop security software leverages new security features in the Intel instruction set to open a virtual compartment to contain each application or e-mail attachment or browser window a user instantiates. Each is akin to a mini quarantined sandbox. Application firewalls from companies like Palo Alto Networks are another advancement providing further protections to the enterprise. The world is constantly changing as to what secure means. As new technologies come online, traditional objections to cloud computing are losing their validity. The FUD [fear, uncertainty, doubt] factors are being addressed by technological innovation.

How will the increasing popularity of mobile devices impact the utilization of cloud computing?

The "consumerization of IT," as commonly referred to in the trade, has been a major development in that users are setting their enterprise IT expectations based upon the experiences they enjoy at home. As users enjoy the wondrous advancements in utility and enjoyment provided by consumer devices and web services from the likes of Google and Apple, they continuously ratchet up their expectations (often unrealistically) upon their internal IT departments. They want to tap into the application universe and do so with location-independent, open network access. Cloud offerings are built to be highly accessible and so in this area, clouds are a natural fit.

How can cloud computing help manage the problem of Big Data?

Cloud simply reduces the barriers to accessing the latest enhancements in the Big Data world. Traditional approaches to implementing such technologies called for supercomputer scale investments, which entail millions of dollars in outlays and implementation times that span quarters. Today, the power and functionality needed to process extremely large datasets are available immediately with no fixed investment required. Innovators like CycleComputing (http://blog.cyclecomputing.com/) are helping life-sciences startups perform millions of hours of computing in days for a few thousand dollars.

The problem with Big Data is the cost. Not only do the kit and software entail expense but also, more importantly, technology managers must consider the cost and difficulty of amassing the required skills to build and continually refine and further develop the platform. The task is daunting. Merely keeping tabs on the technologies available can be a full-time job. The NoSQL sector has myriad choices including Hadoop, MondoDB, Cassandra, and Storm. The storage vendor space is a sea of venture capital–backed innovators that are continually being devoured by the likes of EMC, Hewlett-Packard, Dell, and IBM. Predicting winners and avoiding being stranded on a losing technology is a high-risk game.

Cloud providers not only leverage their scale advantages to make necessary investments; they also absorb risk. Do-it-yourselfers need to make large-scale sunk investments that they will be saddled with for years. Conversely, cloud adopters will enjoy far lower switching costs with a purely variable consumption model. Being able to switch more easily, or walk away from past choices, is a tremendous benefit to the customer.

How did Hurricane Sandy affect cloud computing's image?

In my estimation, cloud computing affected many people on a very personal level when Sandy struck, as it did with many other recent natural disasters. Fred Wilson, the famed venture capitalist, had a wonderful blog post on this subject (www.avc.com/a_vc/2012/11/disaster-and-the-cloud.html). He pointed out that just a few years back he had an extensive IT infrastructure in his basement, which he had recently transitioned to cloud, all of which would have been ruined in the storm had he not. He stressed that the impact would have been not only more costly but far more disruptive if flooding would have claimed all his financial records, not to mention his personal photos and music. One of his portfolio companies had not adopted cloud and spent those first few days feverishly moving into Amazon's cloud where, I suspect, they will remain. At OptionsIT we recently blogged (http://options-it.tumblr.com/post/37332676353/options-pipe-platform-weathers-hurricane-sandy-with) on the fact that the nature of our cloud platform, with component level resiliency across regions, allowed us to operate without any customer disruption, despite the fact that we had just expanded into new offices in New York City that very same weekend that Sandy made landfall! My impression is that Sandy was a tragic wake-up call, one that proved in many cases how indispensable the cloud model has become.

Is the financial services sector leading technological development?

In the past, financial services drove technological development in a variety of areas. We are no longer the alpha dog. The banking industry used to be among a select few industries that possessed IT budgets capable of supporting large-scale R&D. That role reversal does have some advantages in that now we benefit from technology that has been purpose built for other industries but that can be applied to our problems with terrific, lower-cost results.

In your opinion, what is the next "quantum leap" in technology that will revolutionize our industry?

As more people become cognizant of the economics of the infrastructure as service model and cloud computing matures, it will become unthinkable to do business any other way, in certain areas, that is. The nature of the cloud and the significantly reduced time to market that it offers mean that the industry will be able to innovate in a much more rapid manner.

That is not all good news. Widespread cloud adoption will drive the costs of doing business down and reduce barriers of entry to such an extent that competition will increase.

Key Learning Points

- Properly implemented, a cloud solution can more closely align infrastructure expenses with revenues, reduce time to deployment of additional capacity, and reduce the cost of IT operations.

- Reducing the latency of virtualized environments is a major challenge that cloud providers need to meet. On shared servers, users deal with the reality of a shared environment: You may not be first in line. One way to get around this problem is by exposing more controls that allow users to specify affinity, or instructions that specify "control of this CPU will not be ceded to any other application."

- Cloud providers not only leverage their scale advantages to make necessary investments; they also absorb risk. Do-it-yourselfers need to make large-scale sunk investments that they will be saddled with for years. Conversely, cloud adopters will enjoy far lower switching costs with a purely variable consumption model.

CHAPTER 8

Globalization and Automation

Unfinished Business

Technology globalized the financial markets, making it possible for market participants to exploit alpha opportunities across international markets. The automation of trade processes and electronic trading permits market participants to replicate their strategies in new markets rapidly and at lower cost, enabling them to capitalize on market opportunities quickly, wherever they arise.

Globalization and automation are trends that are intertwined; their impact upon financial markets cannot be underestimated. By facilitating democratized access to global markets, automation is in large part responsible for the decentralized nature of many electronically traded markets today. As a byproduct of the greater access that it enables, the number of participants has increased and as a result, markets are arguably more liquid.

As Justin Llewellyn-Jones of Fidessa Corporation relates in this chapter, the trends have farther to run. Automation and a global structure are not characteristic of all markets. For firms that are active in multiple asset classes, the greater use of technology to optimize business processes in more markets has the potential to dismantle more barriers of entry and in the process bring about similar advances in market quality in new products as well.

Globalization requires more than just technology, though technology is a key component. Immense regulatory and other barriers in some markets, which include taxes, capital inflow requirements, [and] even local knowledge of companies, are important factors that determine the pace of international integration. Further, global brokers often use their own international presences and synthetic instruments such as equity swaps or ETFs to facilitate trading on these markets. In this way, they facilitate investment on a global scale and at the same time slow down the globalization process as firms can get access to new markets without "leaving home."

However, a global, interconnected marketplace and greater automation throughout the trade process also introduce challenges for firms on the technology front (for example, greater infrastructure costs). This chapter will discuss how the market utilizes technology to participate in global markets as well as how firms are coping with the associated challenges.

■ Justin Llewellyn-Jones, Fidessa Corporation

Justin Llewellyn-Jones is chief operating officer at Fidessa Corporation and managing director of Fidessa's U.S.–hosted services business. He runs the company's U.S. operations, including software as a service (SaaS) solutions, R&D, operations, infrastructure, and client services. Prior to his current role, Mr. Llewellyn-Jones was senior vice president of service delivery for Fidessa's U.S.–hosted services business. He holds a law degree from the University of Manchester, and a master's in computing from Cardiff University.

Globalization and automation have shaped today's financial markets. Do these trends have farther to run?

While markets have achieved a great deal with respect to globalization and automation, there is still a long road ahead. Segments such as the futures markets demonstrate how far the industry can progress towards a fully automated, global approach, while other segments such as fixed income and other Over-the-Counter (OTC) markets are limited by their lack of transparency and automation. Transparency and risk control, in this case introduced by the new global regulatory mandate for the clearing of OTC transactions, will drive further automation in those markets.

In theory, the automation of human processes is only really limited by desire. As might be expected, entrenched interests are one major deterrent to greater automation as they eliminate human jobs in certain areas. In addition, financial market examples have shown that as greater levels of automation reduce the cost of doing business, more competitors enter markets.

Being able to effectively identify and capitalize on international relationships [between markets] will assume greater importance going forward as firms embrace data to a greater extent as a driver of trading and investment decisions. The industry is paying a great deal of attention to Big Data and the analytics involved in navigating the huge amounts of data available with the goal of finding actionable data items that can improve results and drive those same relationships.

> Being able to effectively identify and capitalize on international relationships [between markets] will assume greater importance going forward as firms embrace data to a greater extent as a driver of trading and investment decisions.

What barriers are left in the global marketplace? How can technology help market participants address them?

Ten years ago, the technological lift required for a given broker to be able to access international markets was formidable, and only those elite firms with sizeable budgets were capable of implementing a global strategy, or even accessing more than a few core markets. Today, many of those international markets are fully electronic and, as a result, are being traded around the clock by market participants in geographically disparate locations. The cost of entry has also dropped dramatically, partly attributed to falling technology costs and partly because technology vendors have been able to deliver economies of scale that allow their customers to access global opportunities at a fraction of what a do-it-yourself solution might cost.

Despite the fact that technology has accomplished a great deal, it is not the lone driver of a global marketplace. It has enabled access to markets around the world, to price data and information, and in doing so has given the financial services community myriad different ways to implement trading strategies including the use of algorithms, analytics, and low-latency networks. However, innovation is hampered when confronted by the business challenges posed by the complex and continually changing global regulatory environment. The international regulatory landscape remains fragmented, dynamic, and uncertain. Dealing with regulations that vary greatly on a country-by-country basis requires firms to maintain expert understanding of the nuances of each market's structure and demands, which places a significant strain on resources. Regulatory certainty would drive globalization forward.

How essential has the adoption of standards like the Financial Information eXchange Protocol (FIX) been in connecting markets on a global scale?

When any industry adopts a standard methodology for communications it triggers a fundamental shift in the barriers to entry to that industry segment. By adopting FIX, the financial services community has enabled participation in the global markets by significantly reducing the cost associated with accessing and transacting business in those markets that have adopted standards.

Standards democratize markets in that they make it both easier and cheaper to trade. In the absence of standards, firms would still participate in global markets. However, the number of participants would shrink since only those with the wherewithal and expertise to comprehend the proprietary landscape, typically the elite and well-capitalized firms, would be able to navigate the domain. Technology can therefore be seen as a great equalizer, putting tools and applications in the hands of more market participants and allowing them to pursue strategies that mimic or perhaps even improve upon the strategies of their larger peers.

FIX has been essential in connecting brokers to brokers, and brokers to clients. In many cases, participants obtain access to markets through member brokers, and in these cases FIX has made electronic connectivity possible, reducing the cost of connection and introducing concepts such as direct market and direct strategy access, leaving the broker's clients with the point of view that they are in fact trading directly into the marketplace.

Looking out on the horizon, how will technology facilitate global trading and investment?

Data is key in this area. Standardization will allow institutional investors and professional traders to look at the characteristics of a trade or investment (e.g., focus on the risk/return ratio) instead of forcing them to decode data in order to be able to identify market opportunities. Standardization will also speed the time to market for new strategies. Data visualization will also result in some fundamental changes. As business intelligence and visualization tools become better at aggressing the huge amount of data that is available, isolating data items that are both valuable and actionable, the comfort level with global markets, both developed and emerging/frontier, will rise.

Has technology reduced or increased the risk for global firms?

Technology is a double-edged sword. By introducing standardization and automation across functions such as data and market access, and by capturing market micro structure regionalization and regulatory nuances, technology will absolutely reduce the cost of entering a market, and in so doing will reduce the operational risks. Nevertheless, the very act of entering the market introduces additional risks to the participant, a simple example being counterparty risk, that can only be offset through knowledge and understanding of that market and its participants.

Technology cannot be seen as a panacea to risk. And despite the reduced operational risks, a global technology footprint certainly introduces more risk on the technology side, as the number and complexity of systems are multiplied. There, proprietary or vendor-supplied automated risk checks and monitoring systems are essential. Firms like Fidessa that can provide proven turnkey solutions can help firms proactively address technology risk both in the tools that they offer and also the long-term experience that they provide. This may be especially important for firms that are just entering a new market.

Finally, as technology enables more firms to operate on a global scale the risk that a firm loses its competitive edge more quickly increases as well.

Has increased automation made markets safer? How?

Again, technology can be seen as both a positive and negative factor. A key contributor to market safety is the electronic audit trail. With an electronic record, events and data can be systematically interrogated pre- and post-trading, which directly leads to greater levels of transparency. Two good examples of where transparency has improved markets are in the areas of price and spreads.

However, technology has allowed for the automation of an ever increasingly complex marketplace, and as we have seen over the last few years, issues with technology can have marked impacts on markets and their participants.

Also, while the added transparency of electronic trading is positive, technology has also contributed to the challenge of Big Data. Increased data volumes are accompanied by, or even caused by, increased speed. The time frames within which events and data need to be interrogated are much reduced, and the sheer amount of data that requires analysis is vast. Nevertheless, further automation, in this case of data analysis, is the only way that systematic checks and balances can be realistically be applied, given the size and complexity of strategies, and markets in general.

How important is the ability to scale in global markets?

Market participants' ability to scale their strategies is an essential factor that will drive further globalization. As more global markets develop deeper liquidity pools that are able to accommodate algorithmic (and other) strategies, they will attract and retain a larger international participant base.

From a business operational standpoint, the automation of trade processes has facilitated firms' ability to scale their operations within markets and across borders. For example, technology enables a single person to service a global clientele and trade in local markets around the world. A single desk can be staffed 24/7.

Where does automation reach its limits?

Especially in areas where complex workflows or calculations exist, the incentives to introduce greater levels of automation are compelling. Automation drives productivity and improves efficiency, thereby reducing costs. However, technology has its limits. The importance of interpersonal relationships and human capital in general in financial markets cannot be underestimated. The examples are myriad.

For one, regional expertise and local relationships are still fundamental for buy-sides when they decide where to route flow and with which broker they transact. In another example that references global markets in particular, emerging markets are one prime example where relationships in combination with cultural insight are of the utmost importance.

Markets around the world are highly regionalized and many need specific functionality and/or localization to make them appeal to local customers. In these markets it may make sense to partner with the right technology partner, as it can help address cultural and linguistic challenges. As a global firm, we invest a great deal into making our products attractive to local audiences. We design them to understand local rules and regulations as well as cultural nuances.

How is technology the enabler of simultaneous globalization and an increase in market fragmentation?

Technology has enabled market participants to apply their trading strategies to markets around the world in a way that was impractical or even impossible in the past. Today's trading strategies can be diverse and complex, the success of which is sometimes completely dictated by technology. The general trend in the industry is toward globalization as technology reduces or even removes barriers to entry. As a result, markets become "closer" or more intertwined as more participants operate across borders.

What one might view as the antithesis of globalization, market fragmentation, also has been driven by technology, but in combination with political will, as in the case of U.S. equity markets. In fact, one can even argue that fragmentation has been a technology-enabled trend, as it is only viable if market participants have technologies such as market data consolidation, ultra-low latency data transmission, and smart order routers to stitch the fragmented world back together. Today, if you want to buy Microsoft in the United States, you need to look at many venues, including exchanges and broker dark pools. None of these venues want to lose their flow since it generates revenue and constitutes their control. Even if technology could solve this by offering perhaps a single global order book for Microsoft, the owners of this liquidity wouldn't agree to share it freely. Before engineering can help, we need to establish the incentives or regulation needed to open up this liquidity.

How is technology helping global firms deal with rapidly increasing levels of market data?

Markets like U.S. equity options dwarf most global markets in terms of the market data that they generate and the demands they place on firms that need it. Of course, storage is a consideration, but the bigger challenge is obtaining globally consistent, time-sensitive, normalized real-time data. In addition to established markets, new and innovative financial products (Exchange Traded Funds [ETFs], derivatives), global participation, and automated trading strategies themselves all contribute to increasing levels of market data, and the velocity of Big Data is only increasing.

Still, this data is absolutely essential. Trading is about correlation. Traders want more data to correlate, for the purposes of both historical testing and real-time trading. Technology will help market participants meet the Big Data challenge in two ways. Performance advances in hardware, networking, and software all support the ability to distribute, capture, process, and/or display market data and keep pace with ever-increasing volume, latency, and storage requirements. However, intelligent analytics that can make sense of massive data sets are currently not yet widely available, and this represents an area of opportunity.

Specifically, vendor technology is useful for firms that are active on a global scale, as it allows these firms to receive normalized global data and participate in global markets with minimal costs. The outsourcing model and its benefits are especially beneficial in the case of global market data.

Will cloud computing be a major factor driving globalization?

Firms are hungry for a unified, global trading platform that facilitates global expansion in a risk-controlled environment. Vendors are responding to this by designing, developing, and delivering these types of cloud (hosted) solutions.

As hosted technology models evolve (e.g., infrastructure as service [IaaS], software as a service [SaaS], data as a service [DaaS]) into global solutions, there will be many more examples of cloud computing supporting global businesses. Currently there are virtually no hosted solutions that holistically support a global business, but we are not too far away from this becoming a reality. Just as vendor-hosted solutions today allow mid- and even small-tier brokers to offer more services to their clients, including algo trading, smart order routing (SOR), program trading, and the capacity to be active in global markets, vendors are also beginning to support global expansion into new and emerging markets.

Though specific concerns with regard to cloud technology remain, they are being addressed. Technology and the service around the technology is now at a point where a wide range of participants of varying sizes and levels of sophistication can consume this "product" with limited operational risk at a sensible price point. The desire for lower and lower latency access to markets, which means colocation or proximity hosting, is now rapidly becoming the norm for certain participant types and will drive the adoption of cloud computing because the cloud offers a cost-effective and flexible way for businesses to become global.

What kind of an advantage can a vendor solution offer versus proprietary technology?

At Fidessa technology is our core competency; it is not a cost of doing business, or a facilitator to our main business lines; it is our core business and the sole source of our revenues. That necessitates a level of expertise and understanding that many firms cannot achieve or cannot afford to acquire. It also means that we will continually look to innovate and improve the products and services we are bringing to the marketplace.

A firm with the scale of Fidessa is exposed to a wide range and large number of different participants, which gives us exposure to many different perspectives. As a result, we can aggregate their needs and visions, and incorporate them into our own. Net-net, we can produce new technologies that meet participants' needs at a cost point that is markedly lower than that which they could achieve on their own.

There will always be a place for proprietary technologies, and it is up to vendors to produce frameworks and Application Programing Interfaces (APIs) that enable firms to preserve their own IP, while leveraging aspects of vendor solutions as part of their mission critical systems. Technology is a broad category and much of the technology that market participants require is not of a privileged nature; it is about sensibly solving well-known problems. In this way, vendors help their customers achieve operational efficiency, which is a different objective than increasing alpha and showing value.

Are advances in technology helping firms deal with increasing global regulatory oversight?

Advances in visualization and data management/standardization are key in helping the market achieve regulatory compliance. The amount of information that is associated with the billions of transactions that occur each and every day makes the job of compliance fantastically difficult. Gathering, aggregating, and storing the data in a form that is accessible is only the starting point. Luckily, the business intelligence data warehouses (BIDWs) of the financial services segment are able to harness the advances in database technology that have been from global powerhouses like Google and Facebook that also have to deal with tremendously large, and ever increasing, data volumes.

Is a standard regulatory and compliance system the answer to addressing the challenge?

Given the scale of the challenge, creating a proprietary system is probably cost prohibitive, so a vendor solution sounds ideal. However, given the multi-asset dimension of some of the oversight now required (e.g., risk), many vendors would not be able to cope with that expansive need. Another factor inhibiting a global approach is that regulation itself is far from global. Country-specific regulations introduce complexity, and this is unlikely to change. A single, "all-powerful" system would be a fantastic boon to the industry, but for now it is a problem domain that is too difficult to resolve with a one-size-fits-all approach. So the challenge then moves to the vendor being able to create a technological framework, essentially doing as much of the heavy lifting as possible, while allowing the participant to configure and customize as necessary.

How long does a technology edge last these days?

The financial services technology world is relatively small and many innovations are rapidly copied, emulated, and adopted almost as soon as they are released. There has also tended to be something of a collaborative approach to technology, with a view that collective adoption of technology that automates workflow is good for everyone.

How does new technology cross your radar?

As a software company, we are focused on innovation. In fact, roughly 20 percent of our own spend is reinvested in R&D each year. Because the financial services technology world is not very large, and the professional network within that segment is very close-knit, we are exposed to ideas via our clients, vendors, peers, and competitors on a daily basis.

We coalesce all of these external ideas with our own vision of where the market is developing. We focus on identifying and subsequently developing and deploying the technological pieces that will facilitate that evolution. At the same time, we are interested in innovation that is occurring on other industry segments and their applicability into financial services. Obvious examples are hardware components like GPUs and FPGAs, unstructured databases in the Big Data space being pursued by the likes of Google and Facebook, microwaves in the telecoms space, and so forth. We get exposure to this space exactly because we're a software company and not a bank.

What would you list as the most important technological achievement within the financial services industry within the last several years? How has it been a game changer?

Being able to apply Big Data concepts across multiple markets, assets, and geographies to determine correlation has been an important recent technological achievement. While correlation studies have existed for quite a while, the capacity of current systems to run global correlations has been propelled by advances in processing power.

In your opinion, what is the next "quantum leap" in trading technology that will revolutionize our industry?

In the markets, the next quantum leap will be the application of technology to new asset classes—for example, the electronification of cash fixed income. The "holdouts" against electronic trading will experience the same levels of efficiency that are currently present in listed derivatives, for example. This will enable firms to become truly global multi-asset, to achieve a truly correlated investment system. This automation of additional markets will break down the remaining barriers, link up markets in much more efficient manner, and drive globalization—and opportunity—to new levels.

What lessons do you have for technologists in our industry?

Technologists should never get complacent, nor should anyone for that matter. Technologists should be careful that they do not just react to the market but also shape it.

Foresight is another important characteristic. Build for growth. At Fidessa, we have grown into different geographies, assets, and segments because our foundation, which is our architecture, allows for expansion. If your architecture is not sound, then you will limit your growth. Similarly, if you outgrow your architecture, build a new one.

Much of the technology that we create brings about structural change. Especially in this area, it does not suffice just to be a good "techie." Technologists need to understand the business and its objectives in order to solve problems. Only when you understand the business can you create your own vision and independent view of the wider market, which lays a strong foundation for personal and corporate success.

 ## Key Learning Points

- By introducing standardization and automation across functions such as data and market access, and by capturing market structure regionalization and regulatory nuances, technology will absolutely reduce the cost of entering a market, and in so doing will reduce the operational risks. Nevertheless, the very act of entering the market introduces additional risks to the participant, a simple example being counterparty risk, that can only be offset through knowledge and understanding of that market and its participants. Technology cannot be seen as a panacea to risk.

- Market participants' ability to scale their strategies is an essential factor that will drive further globalization. As emerging and frontier markets develop more sophisticated structures that are able to accommodate algorithmic (and other) strategies, they will attract and retain a larger international participant base.

- Especially in areas where complex workflows or calculations exist, the incentives to introduce greater levels of automation are compelling. Automation drives productivity and improves efficiency, thereby reducing costs. However, technology has its limits. The importance of interpersonal relationships and human capital in general in financial markets cannot be underestimated.

CHAPTER 9

Room for Improvement in Risk Control

A s the industry employs more technology, we are obligated to ensure that we keep it under control. Runaway algorithms, fat finger errors, as well as non-technology risks like bad actors, are all potential sources of market destabilization. Here, the answer lies in a combination of technology and human oversight. In this chapter, Mark Gorton of Tower Research Capital, a hedge fund, argues that technology has helped to create a fairer, more transparent marketplace than ever before. But that, as an industry, we must deploy a hybrid approach of centrally applied automated risk controls and human vigilance to ensure that the quality of global financial markets continues to improve.

81

▦ Mark Gorton, Tower Research Capital

Managing director Mark Gorton worked in the proprietary trading department of Credit Suisse First Boston where he traded for four and a half years and built sophisticated tools used to analyze the markets. In spring 1998, he left Credit Suisse First Boston to set up Tower Research Capital LLC. Mr. Gorton's professional and educational background provides an unusual combination of math skills and financial knowledge to create and orchestrate the trading strategies utilized at Tower. He has been involved in a number of technology ventures, including Limewire, that are unrelated to financial markets.

How are you implementing technology innovations in a broader sense?

As a trading firm, we opportunistically implement technology as appropriate for our business. Our staff is comprised of individuals with computer-science backgrounds including some with expertise in hardware development. Most of our ideas come from in-house, but that's not to say that we don't keep our eyes open for promising technologies.

What would you list as the most important technological achievement within the financial services industry within the last several years? How has it been a game changer?

There haven't really been any game changing technological advances in the recent past. Technology is always progressing. The huge change was the introduction of electronic trading. Now advances in technology are subtler. Computers become faster. Lines can handle more capacity. I would say that strides are being made in process efficiency. We are maturing as an industry.

What do you believe is your biggest technological achievement, and how has it affected the market?

Our business is more systems integration. As a high-frequency trading (HFT) firm, we have to get a lot of little steps right, including but not limited to technology. There is not one really big thing that determines success or failure. That would be too easy.

Can you talk about speed?

Of course speed is important, but it is just one of many variables that you have to get right in the equation. Speed is an underlying factor in how markets behave, and how they have always behaved. People get worked up about the speed issue, but it's always been a factor in the competitive trading environment. Fast used to mean standing in a good spot in the trading pit. The Rothschilds used carrier pigeons. There's a lot of misinformation or misunderstanding out there with regard to the importance of speed.

Technology has made the markets more egalitarian. Even for the retail investor. Brokers have invested in technology that lets you sit at home and access the markets. Before the advent of electronic trading there was no way that you could be on par with traders in the pits. It was impossible for smaller investors to trade without an intermediary.

Within the trade cycle where will technology have the biggest impact within the next several years and how?

As incremental improvements in technology occur there will be improvements throughout the trade cycle. Where the industry *should* apply technology to make the biggest impact is in risk management. Risk management systems need to be up to the task of handling the complexity of the markets and the sophistication of market participants and their strategies. And currently they're not there.

Where the industry *should* apply technology to make the biggest impact is in risk management.

How can increasing automation in risk management make markets safer?

The markets overall still do not have comprehensive risk systems in place. Automated risk controls can and should feature prominently in a multi-layer risk management system. We should have stringent risk standards in place across the industry. It should be the highest priority for the industry as a whole.

The industry needs to implement best practices and risk control policies for customer order execution algorithms. Automatic shutoffs should be mandated for order execution algorithms that stop trading in the event of a large market move. At that point, you should have people take a look to make sure everything is okay before restarting the algorithms. During the Flash Crash a huge sell order was being processed by an order execution algorithm. It kept robotically selling into a freefalling market, causing giant market disturbances. This was the major problem with the Flash Crash, and it was identified years ago, but nothing has been done to make sure that this sort of problem does not repeat itself. So it would be great to have a thorough set of risk controls mandated for every customer order execution algorithm.

As an industry, are we relying too much on technology to manage risk?

We need to combine technology with increased human vigilance. The human side of risk management cannot be overlooked. In the days before electronic trading, you had brokers. If the market were in free fall, your broker wouldn't execute your order for you at any price. He would call you and ask you if you still wanted to execute. That human common sense is missing in many cases. It's easy to program that logic, but people need to actually do it.

What should risk standards look like?

As an industry standard there should be three independent layers of risk control: on the trading firm side, in-house at the brokerage firm or clearer, depending on the asset class, and at the exchange level. No market participant, regardless of size or complexity, should be exempt. Right now, two layers are the most that you have. Some market participants take risk seriously and are doing it internally, but you won't get everyone to do so unless you mandate it.

People need to assume that their code is flawed and have systems in place to catch errors when they occur. You cannot produce bug-free code. It's not even possible to be vigilant for a set list of errors because you can't come up with a comprehensive list of what you should be looking for. Code is highly variable.

Exchanges in particular have a responsibility to take part in the risk-control process to protect the markets, and at the moment, they pretty much ignore this responsibility. They need automated controls, and they need good procedures to make sure that they can contact customers in the event of a problem.

What would you say to those that want to limit technological advances in the marketplace (e.g., throttling speed)?

Many in the industry as well as those looking in through the windows highlight speed as a problem that needs to be solved. It's not clear to me that speed is a problem. Technology has driven costs down tremendously. Today we have the lowest transaction costs in the history of the markets, which translates into more people having more capital and retiring with larger savings than ever before. The "good old days" when traders were an entrenched club were much worse for investors. Of course the market structure isn't perfect, but it's the best we've ever had and we can thank technology for that.

Is it harder these days for firms to gain a technology edge given the fact that there are many more technologically savvy trading firms?

It's the same as before. As new technologies or better, more powerful versions of current technology are introduced, we are forced to upgrade to keep pace. Our competitors are in the same boat. To be frank about it, I would prefer if there were no new lines introduced. We would save money by not having to upgrade continuously. But we have to and that's just the cost of doing business. These "updates" may happen at a faster rate than they used to, but fundamentally it's the same process of change.

How long does an IT edge last?

It's hard to say. Months. Maybe a year or two.

Technological innovation undoubtedly happens on the proprietary trading side. Given the importance of secrecy in protecting edge, how does one protect intellectual property (IP)?

The simple answer is that you don't. You work at employee retention. There are other smart people out there who have figured it out, too. You have to keep innovating to retain your competitive edge.

In the development of trading strategies, do you develop hardware as well as software, or is that simply not where your competitive advantage lies?

We program more software than hardware. We purchase from vendors, particularly on the hardware side. Innovation comes from all sides and if there's a better mousetrap in the market, we'll do our due diligence.

Can you provide any insight into how Tower handles the Big Data problem? Are advances in storage technology like solid state drives and tiering being widely adopted to tackle the issue?

We buy lots of technology. Data sets in other industries are much larger, and much more fundamentally important, like in the healthcare industry where you die if mistakes are made. We are able to benefit from their advances.

What keeps you up at night?

Not much keeps me up at the moment. The Knight situation prompted us to review our internal procedures. There will always be errors, but you want redundancy in risk systems.

Can you discuss the demands that the Flash Crash and sovereign debt crisis placed on IT?

We traded though the Flash Crash and sovereign debt crisis. In 2007 and 2008 we experienced huge spikes in volume in the industry. Volumes are low now. We built systems to deal with the kind of traffic that was characteristic of the pre-crisis days. I'd venture a guess and say that very few people are experiencing capacity problems now. As a high-frequency trading firm, we are constantly engineering our systems to handle stress. Sure, we slow down but we address those slowdowns when they happen. They act as an early warning system for us to indicate potential problems. We don't wait until something larger happens to force our hand.

Was high-frequency trading responsible for the Flash Crash?

No. HFT was vilified. They [regulators, politicians, the media] went after HFT but it was really execution algorithms that were responsible, and no one has addressed any of the problems with execution algorithms.

Can you discuss your biggest or a prominent mistake, and how you grew from it as a firm?

Small things happen from time to time. We are concerned when they happen. What we try to promote is a zero-error culture. We want zero trading errors and to prevent them we want to promote a Six Sigma–like mentality. Every small malfunction tells us that there is a problem. You want to drive small errors out of your system because then you are less likely to have big errors.

How do you attract and, importantly, retain the best talent in such a competitive industry? Tower has a unique culture; is the personality of a candidate your highest priority?

Recruiting is very, very hard. We're not only competing with the rest of Wall Street for technologists. We are competing against the likes of Google and Facebook. Treat people well. You'd be hard pressed to find someone in our industry who prioritizes personality over skill but it is an important factor. The technologists at Tower are my kind of people.

 Key Learning Points

- Speed has always been a factor in the competitive trading environment. There is a lot of misinformation or misunderstanding out there with regard to the importance of speed.

- Automated risk controls can and should feature prominently in a multi-layer risk management system. We should have stringent risk standards in place across the industry. It should be the highest priority for the industry as a whole.

- Every small malfunction tells us that there is a problem. You want to drive small errors out of your system because then you are less likely to have big errors.

CHAPTER 10

Trading Systems

Dealing with Velocity

In this chapter, leading technologists from CME Group including chief information officer Kevin Kometer and managing directors David Hoag and Ian Wall discuss their insights on how the industry is harnessing technology to further reduce latency, enhance transactional consistency, as well as make markets safer. Theirs are valuable perspectives on how the industry is dealing with velocity on a variety of levels.

89

Advances in technology, chief among which is the widespread adoption of co-location services, have significantly accelerated the pace of trading; on exchange and alternative trading platforms, in some cases execution takes place on the sub-millisecond level. In just one example, CME Group, a leading provider of listed derivatives across all major asset classes, cites order execution round-trip times of under one millisecond for orders originating from within its co-location facility. Trading is faster than ever before.

Trading systems will continue to become faster as new technologies are introduced. But the relative importance of additional increases in speed may be diminishing. A new trend is emerging in financial services: the prioritization of consistency in round-trip times over further, incremental reductions in latency.

The advantages and disadvantages of the reduction in transactional latency have been hotly disputed. One thing that the financial industry as a whole can agree upon is the need for added safeguards to prevent runaway algorithms and other such accidents. Throughout the trade cycle, systems providers, vendors, and end users are actively developing solutions to meet this challenge.

According to *Automated Trader* magazine's 2011 Algorithmic Trading Survey[*], a growing number of algorithmic traders consider themselves "fast enough" and are choosing to focus on finding alpha in variables other than speed, including smarter algorithms, distributed and collaborative trading intelligence, and implementing increased automation in different areas of the trade cycle.

Now that execution speeds have reached extremely fast levels, consistency in round-trip times has emerged as the new priority for algorithmic traders, as it allows them to better calibrate algorithmic models. Pursuing further reductions in latency is a game of diminishing returns, one many market participants have decided not to play.

Myriad built-in safeguards are already an integral part of today's highest-volume electronic trading systems. These integrated pre-trade risk management tools are growing in complexity to match developments in the markets. Circuit breakers and volatility interruptions have been present in electronic markets in some cases for over 20 years and serve as effective speed bumps. Other, newer additions such as stop buttons allow members to programmatically stop trading activity when certain thresholds are breached. In one exchange's offering, trading activity is linked to available margin deposits.

Protecting the markets from errant technology is a shared responsibility. Risk management system vendors, exchanges, clearinghouses, settlement agencies, and certainly end users all play an important role. This chapter asks the technology leaders within an exchange conglomerate for their opinion on the landscape. As the focal point of electronic transactions, their systems interface with dozens of vendor systems and thousands of customers. Thus, they are well placed to provide a survey of best practices.

In the futures industry, in 2010 the Futures Industry Association's Principal Traders Group published its collective opinion on risk management best practices in a document entitled "Recommendations for Risk Controls for Trading Firms" (www.futuresindustry.org/downloads/Trading_Best_Pratices .pdf). This document provides a concise overview of available system-based risk controls.

Especially for latency-sensitive firms, a point of contention has been where the onus lies in electronic risk management. Should risk controls be optional and as a result penalize those that prudently adopt them, or should certain risk controls be obligatory, thus leveling the playing field for all?

TRADING SYSTEMS

---

[*] *Automated Trader.* "Automated Trader 2011 Algorithmic Trading Survey." Survey. January, 2012.

Currently, risk controls that affect the marketplace on the whole, like those triggered by volatility, are mandatory, while company and trading account specific controls are discretionary.

■ Kevin Kometer, David Hoag, and Ian Wall, CME Group

Kevin Kometer is senior managing director and chief information officer of CME Group. He is responsible for leading CME Group's technology and enterprise computing division. During his tenure, he has led the technology integration efforts following CME's merger with the Chicago Board of Trade (CBOT) in 2007 and CME Group's acquisition of the New York Mercantile Exchange (NYMEX) in 2008. He also is responsible for advancing the global growth of the company's technology infrastructure, including technology distribution for 15 strategic partnerships and 10 telecommunication hubs around the world.

Ian Wall serves as managing director, architecture of CME Group. He is responsible for leading the architecture plans and strategies that enable CME Group to achieve its business goals on an enterprise-wide basis. Before assuming his current role, Wall served as managing director, NYMEX information technology following CME Group's acquisition of NYMEX in 2008.

David Hoag serves as managing director, software engineering of CME Group. He leads a team responsible for post-trade, regulatory, and risk management systems. The delivery of reliable technology solutions enables CME Clearing to protect the integrity of its current markets and expand into new ones.

How has your technology impacted the market?

CME Group's Globex system was one of the first electronic trading systems worldwide. As an early innovator in electronic trading systems, we promoted decentralized access to markets that allowed our customers to manage their risk management needs around the clock. And we've continued to build from there.

In particular, our Drop Copy technology is widely recognized as the gold standard when managing the risk when a given customer's electronic connection to the market is "dropped." Our Drop Copy service sends copies of execution reports, heartbeats and acknowledgments, and trade bust messages through a Financial Information eXchange (FIX) Protocol-based messaging interface. Giving customers the security that they will not miss important trade data was a game changer as more and more firms embraced algorithmic trading. In fact, the term *drop copy* has been co-opted by firms to refer to similar offerings by other exchanges and software vendors.

Are markets fast enough?

No one is arguing the case to abandon further performance enhancements in trading systems. At CME Group, we measure round-trip times at 1.8 milliseconds within our data center and expect to take that down significantly in the near term. What many in the market have come to realize is that, simply put, it is too expensive to get further reductions in latency in relation to what they get in return. Market participants are voicing a preference of predictability, or consistency in round-trip times over added speed—within reason, that is.

What can be done to further reduce latency in trading systems?

If we use the example of our Globex trading system, we continually introduce changes to enhance performance. Figure 10.1 illustrates recent Globex performance enhancements.

We are re-architecting the order entry and market data pieces to bring latency down from an average of 1.8 milliseconds to 600 microseconds. In addition, we are introducing a new network topology that will minimize the number of network hops, which also will deliver substantial performance benefits to our users.

If we take a step back and try to answer the question generically for the industry as a whole, scaling is a way to enhance performance. Everyone in the industry is "scaling it out." Besides the obvious of implementing new technologies like faster servers, data lines, etcetera, technologists in the industry need to think out of the box in terms of programming and networking, just to name a few areas. The easy reductions in latency have been achieved and it is more difficult to deliver additional speed. That is not to say that it cannot be done; it is just a bigger challenge.

Pinpointing the next point of significant latency reduction is difficult. It may be on the analysis side as data management becomes easier through faster processing.

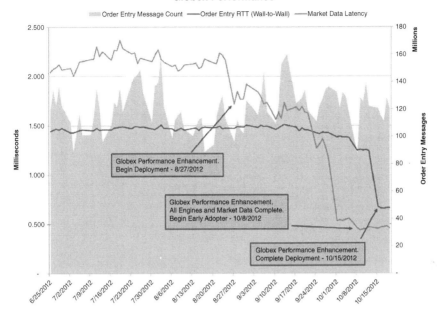

Globex Performance

Order Entry Message Count ——Order Entry RTT (Wall-to-Wall) ——Market Data Latency

Globex Performance Enhancement.
Begin Deployment - 8/27/2012

Globex Performance Enhancement,
All Engines and Market Data Complete.
Begin Early Adopter - 10/8/2012

Globex Performance Enhancement.
Complete Deployment - 10/15/2012

FIGURE 10.1   Reprinted with permission of CME Group.

Why are market participants increasingly focused on consistency?

The edge that market participants once had with speed is diminished and frankly, many market participants weigh the additional cost of incremental reductions in latency and are judging them to be cost-prohibitive. So trading firms are looking for other ways to generate alpha. Consistency is the new watchword because it allows trading firms to better strategize.

> Consistency is the new watchword because it allows trading firms to better strategize.

How does one increase consistency?

The topic of consistency in round-trip times is closely linked to the last question. Our customers are keenly interested in achieving greater levels of consistency in order to better calibrate their models. And as a result of our efforts on that front, Globex is getting faster. Performance improvements become a byproduct of consistency. The aforementioned performance improvements to Globex were targeted at improving consistency, and achieved a 98 percent reduction in latency at the 95th percentile. This also brought about the reduction in median latency to 600 microseconds.

Trading is now ultrafast. How is the market utilizing technology to cope with the increased velocity of trading?

From a business standpoint, market participants recognize the need to deploy proactive risk measures to safeguard the market, and technology enables us to do that. With this joint objective in mind, the industry as a whole is actively utilizing technology to implement system-based risk controls as part of a system of checks and balances on the speed of trading.

To use CME Group as an example, we have a number of automated safeguards on the execution side, including volume controls, circuit breakers to halt markets in extremely volatile market conditions, and message policies to deter excessive activity by trading firms. We also have in place a risk management interface that supports granular, pre-trade risk management for clearing firms.

The good news is that risk management systems directly benefit from advances in trading technology. As an exchange and clearinghouse operator, we are actively leveraging what we implement on the execution side for risk management and clearing systems. Developments in data warehouse appliances, hardware acceleration, and increasing use of the grid approach all benefit risk management systems equally as they do trading systems. As for the competitive landscape, we see this as well with other exchanges and trading systems providers on the listed derivatives side.

How can increasing automation in risk management make markets safer?

The velocity of algorithmic trading makes it virtually impossible for a human to hit the emergency brake in an emergency situation. Increasing the automation in risk controls is needed to keep pace with parallel developments in trading (for example, speeding up controls that pause markets if a volatility threshold is breached or deleting open orders if a connection is lost).

From a technology standpoint, it is a relatively simple process to repurpose trading technology for use in risk management tools. However, there are significant business challenges to increasing the automation in risk management—namely, that you don't know what your customer's global position is and whether it is hedged somewhere else. A big part of the risk management onus lies with global clearing firms.

Utilizing graphical processing unit (GPU) technology in the parallel processing of options pricing is one example in which technology can help make risk-management calculations more efficient. It is a logical step to algorithmically link faster analysis with a faster safety switch.

Can you discuss the technology challenges posed by implementing automated risk controls in multiple markets?

Effective risk management requires risk calculations that span multiple asset classes. For example, a customer may be trading Treasuries against OTC IRS swaps. Imagine the situation where volatility thresholds are breached in Treasury futures. Viewing this market as an independent market, and independently halting trading from the OTC market could increase overall systemic risk by eliminating the ability to hedge OTC IRS positions with futures.

On top of the wide variety of listed derivatives markets that we run, the introduction of electronic OTC clearing has also led to functional complexities as well.

Who are the leaders in automated risk controls?

We think that as the front line, exchanges are in the position to push the development and implementation of automated risk management tools that protect the marketplace. Volatility interruptions and circuit breakers protect the integrity of markets. It is in our best interest to ensure that markets run smoothly.

On the futures side, we have the integrated risk management component of the clearinghouse, and the interplay between the real-time margining and the trading systems strengthens the risk management approach.

When it comes to automated risk tools that protect individual market participants, we see the high-frequency firms in the lead, as their solvency depends on it. Cutoff switches or panic buttons are probably the automated risk-management tool that is most important—and already in use—in virtually all firms that trade algorithmically.

Do you find trading firms to be resistant to automated risk controls?

No, while trading firms are sensitive about additional pre-trade steps that affect their speed and therefore competitiveness, automated risk controls are embraced by almost everyone. It is in their best interest to prevent the "runaway algorithm," not to mention fat finger and other smaller errors.

The Flash Crash was an eye opener for many firms as it underscored the importance of preparedness in terms of preventative risk controls.

How do domestic and international partnerships impact your technology?

In the case of our Brazilian partnership with BM&FBOVESPA, we faced an exciting technology challenge—namely, developing a new platform in a new market segment for us, which is cash equities. The ultra-low latency nature of cash market trading has brought added benefits as well for our core derivatives customers.

Our network of global partnerships and Globex hubs also pushed us to develop a global backbone, which is a low-latency, dark fiber network that is fully controlled and operated by CME Group.

In your opinion, what is the next "quantum leap" in trading technology that will revolutionize our industry?

We are an applied technology company so we scout out technology from other areas rather than building our own, with many exceptions of course. We plug it in and get quick results with minimal time to market. In many cases, and this is how we will answer the question, repurposed technology can have a significant impact on the trading industry. Hardware acceleration, for example, has been around in other industries for a long time but is a game changer in finance. Pre-trade credit controls can be implemented in hardware-accelerated solutions at a fraction of the associated latency of software-only solutions, thus somewhat eliminating any potential concern about speed versus managing risk that some may have.

How are you implementing IT innovations from the broader industry? Do you actively seek out non-financial industry sources?

We have an ongoing commitment to our customers to enhance trading. And with that goal in mind, we actively seek out technologies that positively impact all areas of the trade cycle. In fact, our desire to stay ahead of the game from a technology standpoint is evidenced in what we call our Emerging Technologies Team. It's an interdepartmental team of technology experts whose goals are to provide proof of concepts for new technologies.

There has always been a two-way street in terms of technology development between finance and other areas. Large-scale databases are a good case; most of the developments in that area come from outside finance. In the healthcare, aerospace, and communications industries high-performance solutions are needed to solve complex computational problems, and we certainly benefit from the developments there.

Another area in which we excel is in working with technology vendors, like CISCO, to co-develop products that fit our needs. We follow a collaborative approach.

How do universities or research facilities play a role in your development process?

We recognize that universities with strong financial and economic programs play a critical role in educating both prospective market participants and regulators. Therefore, we continuously explore ways to collaborate with professors that cover our markets, either in the classroom or from a research perspective. To that end, we hold a number of trading competitions.

The CME Group Commodity Trading Challenge is held each year in February and March. This competition is open to both undergraduate and graduate students and is focused on our crude oil and gold futures.

We also sponsor the Tulane University Energy Trading Competition held each year in September and October. This is a risk-adjusted electronic trading competition focusing on crude oil and natural gas futures. It is open to both undergraduate and graduate students.

From its start at the University of Houston over a decade ago, the CME Group Commodity Trading Challenge has grown into a global competition, involving over 750 undergraduate and graduate students from 95 universities. It is now global in its reach with schools from Canada, Germany,

England, India, Poland, Italy, and Greece. The Challenge has two components: electronic trading and open outcry. This event gives the students tremendous exposure to what trading is like on a professional platform and a better understanding for how the markets react in real time.

Do you have any special lessons for technologists?

Technology is a fast-paced industry. New solutions, methodologies, and practices present themselves almost daily. It is important for a technologist to remember the drivers behind a particular solution, rather than become beholden to a particular solution. The drivers themselves must be revisited as technology and the finance industry evolve over time. An openness to continually explore new technologies and the value they can bring the business must be maintained, even if they may be disruptive to the technology department.

 Key Learning Points

- The velocity of algorithmic trading makes it virtually impossible for a human to hit the emergency brake in an emergency situation. Increasing the automation in risk controls is needed to keep pace with parallel developments in trading.

- As the front line, exchanges are in the position to push the development and implementation of automated risk management tools that protect the marketplace. Volatility interruptions and circuit breakers protect the integrity of markets.

- What many in the market have come to realize is that, simply put, it is too expensive to get further reductions in latency in relation to what they get in return. Market participants are voicing a preference of predictability, or consistency in round-trip times over added speed—within reason, that is.

CHAPTER 11

Technology and Alternatives

Benefits of Better Data

Today's data management challenges, discussed in depth in another chapter, are centered around logistical concerns and the extraction of value from massive quantities of both structured and unstructured data. In this chapter, William Murphy of The Blackstone Group shares his perspectives on another component of the Big Data challenge: data management in illiquid alternative investment products. User-friendly solutions to facilitate data collection have helped firms like Blackstone leverage technology to gather high-quality data from portfolio companies and, in the process, set new standards for transparency in the alternatives industry.

Data is at the core of contemporary markets. Frankly, it's always been the foundation for trading and investment decisions. In a mirror of general societal trends, capital markets are also experiencing a tremendous growth in data generation. Smart technologists regard this growth as a key opportunity and are innovating in the area of data management. Their technology solutions help market participants both gather and tap into new sources of data.

Better-quality, more comprehensive data in all markets, listed and OTC, is a contemporary trend, partly driven by regulation and partly the result of investor expectations with regard to transparency. Greater insights into these markets is ushering in a range of benefits for managers as well as end investors. Chief among them are superior pre and post-trade analysis, enhanced transparency, and optimized risk management.

■ William Murphy, The Blackstone Group

William Murphy is the chief technology officer at Blackstone, leading the Blackstone innovations and infrastructure team. He is responsible for the firm's technology efforts. Prior to joining Blackstone in 2011, Bill was founding chief technology officer for Capital IQ. There, he was responsible for overseeing all product design, development, infrastructure, and technology support, and was involved with all operations of the business.

Before Capital IQ, Bill led teams at Sapient, delivering solutions for large clients primarily in financial services. He received a BSE in computer science from the University of Pennsylvania.

What are the special challenges posed by data collection in alternative assets?

Data collection and standardization are the chief problems in alternatives. Data quality is essential in that high-quality data provides the business side with the best possible foundation for decision making. People tend to focus instead on analysis tools full of bells and whistles. However, without quality data, analytics fail to give users true insights and even have the potential to mislead. The collection process is often difficult, especially for private equity, where data is collected from private companies in geographically disparate locations. We utilize a product from iLevel Solutions to streamline the process and make our valuation process more effective.

> **Without quality data, analytics fail to give users true insights and even have the potential to mislead.**

The more data that we and other firms collect in the area of alternatives drives cost down throughout the firm by making our professionals more effective. High-quality data adds value in a variety of areas including risk management and pre-trade analytics.

How are you harnessing technology to facilitate data collection?

Specifically for valuations, in iLevel Solutions, we have developed and deployed a data aggregation platform to pull data into a repository. The CFOs of our portfolio companies enter data in Excel and submit it to Blackstone for review and approval. In rolling out the software, we introduced greater automation and streamlined processes. As a result of simplifying the data gathering process from a technical standpoint, we reduced manual error, thus enhancing overall data quality. We couple this data with other publicly available and privately available information to compile our full risk picture. Having the ability to centralize to a single version of the truth is critical to using the data effectively across the firm.

How are new technologies helping to increase transparency for investors?

Technology alone cannot enhance transparency. Our users and the business must embrace it in order to provide our investors with the information they require. We feel this is an area for innovation in the industry and want to lead the way.

At Blackstone we provide our investors with data and secure documents through our investor portal. The portal allows them to drill into their investments and the underlying portfolio assets that make up the funds.

Leaving technology aside, behavioral changes are helping generate increased transparency in alternative asset classes. In part, the push can be linked to high-visibility scandals in the broader financial markets that have prompted regulators to increase scrutiny. Even in the absence of regulatory reform, for the most part, firms generally are beginning to recognize the value in being more open.

However, people's increasing acceptance of technology in general may be a greater reason why markets are embracing greater levels of transparency. Simply, people are more accustomed to transparency in other areas of their lives and they recognize the benefits. Alternatives should keep pace.

How are advances in technology improving risk management generally?

Increases in processing power and data availability are helping companies to better, and more rapidly, assess risk. It is a two-lever approach: having the best data available and making the best insights based on that data. We work diligently to categorize data and to build relevant data sets. Technology is the enabler of that.

As an industry, are we relying too much on technology when managing risk?

Some level of automation in risk systems is desirable, but important decisions cannot and should not be completely outsourced to artificial intelligence. Advances in technology are enabling people to make risk decisions more efficiently. Blackstone relies on clear heads with the right data to assess our risks all the time.

Greater utilization of technology introduces a new risk. As a result, the importance of quality software is heightened. Technology managers increasingly need to focus on promoting "zero error" cultures in order to avoid problems. An associated risk to that is technology talent management. Once you have achieved best-in-class software, you must continuously fine-tune systems as markets change. If you have employee attrition, your job becomes more difficult. For technology managers, contingency planning in this area is essential, especially in today's competitive [technology] jobs market. We have a growing problem: the introduction of a new risk coupled with a dearth of talent available in the market.

How does technology help you compile a complete risk picture?

It seems that for many people, there is a desire to boil risk down to one number. In our case, we present information in the best way possible and let smart, experienced people look at it.

In financial markets, we have a special challenge because we are interconnected to massive numbers of other systems, which must be pieced together to provide a comprehensive picture. We follow a hybrid approach by combining in-house and vendor systems. In my experience, one-size-fits-all never works.

We buy what we can, we build what we need and then glue all of the pieces together for maximum efficiency. Generally, the product companies in any industry wind up leading in the area of development since they can invest more across many clients and benefit from economies of scale.

How did the financial crisis impact the importance of risk management for technologists?

It should always have been high. The key is fostering a partnership between the technology and business sides. This is true in all areas, but the financial crisis has brought risk management to the forefront. It is certainly more important than five years ago.

The underpinnings of successful risk management also help propel other initiatives and even generate new ideas. For instance, we mastered our entities for the express purpose of enhancing risk management, but that process has allowed us to build efficiencies in our tax processes and in a variety of other areas.

How are you using new technology to help secure data?

One example is that we use third-party software to help deal with the challenges posed by mobile technology. As tablet use expanded, like most people, we were nervous about what happens when sensitive data leaves the Blackstone ecosystem. We opted to adopt WatchDox, which enables document protection across a variety of devices and use cases. It is a very robust solution that lets us keep a close handle on our sensitive documents. It makes sense to balance accessibility with security because we want our staff to be able to access the tools they need, albeit in a secure way.

How important are processes in maintaining IT excellence in the area of risk management?

Standardization of data and technology is vital. It ensures that you have a well-conceived plan for implementation and maintenance of software and hardware. It also lowers maintenance costs and risks associated with technology sprawl.

Sometimes, people view standardization as bureaucracy, but if done right, employees benefit from following institutionalized processes as they can be more efficient and repeatable. It comes down to fostering a culture that builds innovation in a way that is sustainable by creating standardized building blocks that enable projects to come together both faster and more reliably.

How does new technology cross your radar?

Staying current has become one of the hardest things to do because of the pace of innovation. Maintaining an active role in industry organizations is helpful, and we are lucky that a good camaraderie exists among financial technologists. In other industries, technology is such a core part of business models that they cannot share insights. In our group, we hear stories where other people have enjoyed successes and failures, and can learn from those. It is a challenge to sort through the noise to find areas that add real value. Often, it is a gradual process of raising the bar for the entire industry.

Is regulatory reform quickening or slowing the pace of technological innovation?

Our goal is to improve ahead of new regulations. We are using the impending changes as a catalyst to make ourselves better where we can. Viewing the work related to regulatory compliance as a positive exercise is important. Regulatory requirements reprioritize some projects from "nice to haves" to "must haves."

What lessons do you have for technologists in our industry?

Many people say that there are parallels between sports and the financial industry, and I emphatically agree. I am an avid runner and a big fan of a book by Christopher McDougall entitled *Born to Run: A Hidden Tribe, Superathletes and the Greatest Race the World Has Never Seen*. In his book he writes, "You don't stop running because you get old; you get old because you stop running." The same is true in technology, and more broadly in business.

If you are a leader, build a culture that rewards innovation in a way that is sustainable. Build a team that is always focused on what they can do to improve, and you will stop any decline to mediocrity. Convincing other business leaders that you are never "finished"—that you need to keep investing in technology—is often difficult, but it is essential. Failure to do so can mean that the technical architecture and organization will get stale and cease to create competitive advantages. In this scenario you also start to lose your best people, and that can create a downward spiral. Avoid it at all costs.

Are you involved in any educational partnerships that aim to foster technological skills in students?

We run a charitable program called The Blackstone Entrepreneurship Foundation, which supports innovative programs that foster entrepreneurship and, in turn, economic growth. The initiative focuses efforts on producing enduring results in geographies hardest hit by the global economic crisis. We are active in a variety of locations. The program, called Blackstone Launch Pad, is a college- and university-based program that treats entrepreneurship as a mainstream career path with the goal of teaching students and alumni how to create jobs, not just find jobs. In addition, at Blackstone technology we are building relationships with the top technology schools to provide a path from those great institutions directly to the financial technology world.

 Key Learning Points

- Increases in processing power and data availability are helping companies to better, and more rapidly, assess risk. It is a two-lever approach: having the best data available and making the best insights based on that data.

- Some level of automation in risk systems is desirable, but important decisions cannot and should not be completely outsourced to artificial intelligence. Advances in technology are enabling people to make risk decisions more efficiently.

- Standardization of data and technology is vital. It ensures that you have a well-conceived plan for implementation and maintenance of software and hardware. It also lowers maintenance costs and risks associated with technology sprawl.

TECHNOLOGY AND ALTERNATIVES

CHAPTER 12

Data Centers

Harnessing Networks

In the recent past, the collective industry decision to co-locate servers in data centers has profoundly impacted transactional speed. But many in the industry have taken a conscious decision to opt out of the latency "race to zero" and are focusing instead on developing alternative ways to generate alpha. The "trading smarter" trend is developing as an increasing number of market participants look to connect to a greater number of data inputs in an effort to enhance pre-trade decision making and gain an information edge. Data centers are cognizant of this sea change and are stepping up to help firms connect to a greater number of sources.

Data centers, especially the successful and densely populated ones, are the brick-and-mortar structures where meetups in the world of electronic markets are occurring. Savvy data centers are looking to utilize this fact to add value for customers. Looking forward, the data center is emerging as a broker of sorts, introducing customers to valuable new business relationships within their existing customer networks. John Knuff of Equinix provides his perspectives on the data center landscape and how they are adding value by fostering relationships between their customers.

Why are data centers so important in today's financial markets? They offer a number of products and services that add value throughout the trade cycle, including co-location and network connectivity. The widespread adoption of the data center model already has tremendously impacted our industry, helping customers streamline business processes, and thus reduce operational costs. An important byproduct is enhanced market stability overall, which is in part achieved by helping to make business continuity services both widely available and affordable.

Traditional exchange trading floors have either declined drastically in importance or disappeared altogether, and data centers have assumed the role of physical meeting point for a wide range of market participants. They are the new Buttonwood Trees.

■ John Knuff, Equinix

John Knuff is the general manager, global financial services for Equinix.

He is responsible for business growth across Equinix's global financial markets division. He and his team regularly advise clients on complex network and systems deployment strategies for their trading infrastructure. A pioneer in global financial ecosystems, John was recently recognized as one of the "Biggest Innovators on Wall Street" by Securities Technology Monitor. Prior to joining Equinix, he was managing director at NYFIX, where he grew the NYFIX network into one of the largest global electronic trading networks, where customers in 21 countries routed hundreds of millions of shares on a daily basis.

How has the data center revolutionized trading?

The data center has emerged as the new Buttonwood Tree. Being adjacent to other traders in the heyday of the pits was very important. In much the same way, computers need to be adjacent to other systems, market data feeds, [and so forth]. As the number of required connection points has grown, our value—and the value of any data center—is now measured in the ability to connect customers to key systems. As trading functions have been transferred from humans to machines, the data center has become a meeting place for computers to meet up easily and without friction.

Data centers provide a number of advantages for market participants, not the least of which is cost savings. By offering a range of services such as disaster recovery, we do our part to enhance overall market safety.

As the number of required connection points has grown, our value—and the value of any data center—is now measured in the ability to connect customers to key systems.

Is data center utilization by firms a must?

Whether a company chooses to utilize a data center depends on its trading styles and how much trading technology it has implemented. Data centers excel at helping trading firms optimize their connectivity to markets and to a variety of other firms. How connected a trading firm believes that it needs to be is what drives a co-location decision.

The decision to utilize a data center for high-frequency trading (HFT) and non-HFT firms alike is often related to fiduciary duty. Guaranteeing uptimes is a key business concern. The safety that a data center offers (physical security, disaster recovery, etc.) often drives a firm's decision. And safety concerns were just underscored with the unfortunate damage caused by Hurricane Sandy.

What is arguably the single greatest value-add of data center usage?

The chief advantage of a data center is its ability to help users save costs. Data centers offer customers the ability to quickly and cost-effectively connect across the aisle to key vendors or customers. Hosting many systems under one roof has changed the economic model and made it possible for firms to expand their networks at a reasonable cost, and at significantly reduced time to market.

As the trading landscape continues to evolve, firms are pressed to maintain connectivity to an increasing number of interfaces, including trading venues, counterparties, vendors, and others. The "trading smart" component for many firms has grown. For most in the industry, it is no longer a question of maintaining connectivity solely to execution venues. In order to remain competitive, firms are obligated to connect to a much greater number of information sources, including newsfeeds and economic data providers. Further complicating matters, firms must manage these myriad connections on a global scale in order to capitalize on market opportunities around the world. As the number of inputs to trading decisions continues to grow, firms require more bandwidth. Implementing these must-haves with a data center drives costs down.

Equinix has a background outside financial services. How has that different background helped you to offer unique products and services to financial customers?

The founders of Equinix envisioned a neutral meeting place for Internet participants. They built the first data center for networks that moved

Internet traffic, known as the "eyeball networks," for consumers as well as the content providers. They sought to offer a neutral environment in which users could exchange data traffic. And one of the reasons that the Internet prospered and continues to prosper is the global network. Early data centers facilitated peering in a neutral peering point. We do the same thing in financial services but we do not refer to it as peering. Equinix's roots in Silicon Valley help to keep us engaged in developing technology trends. We are on the front lines of where contemporary technology innovations are occurring.

How are data centers helping financial firms grow their businesses?

In today's world data centers are the financial industry's electronic meeting points. In a well-populated data center businesses can virtually meet more of their peers and develop joint opportunities for growth. At Equinix, we offer a product called our Ecosystem Visualization Tool, which visually demonstrates to customers how they are interconnected to others in the markets. It helps firms see their upstream connections to vendors, datacenters, info sources, and counterparties. The tool also shows connectivity to trading sites or post-trade services.

Where this program excels is that it also helps customers see other potential new connections within our data center ecosystem. Thus, we facilitate the identification of potential connections to enhance their businesses, whether that be to take in more order flow, destinations to send their orders, and more.

LinkedIn is a good analogy. Much like how LinkedIn suggests new connections for its users, our Ecosystem Visualization Tool visually depicts our customers' first-degree connections and their second-degree connections. Most professionals in the financial services industry intuitively know their peers but once they visualize the ecosystem, it can be an "a-ha moment." We show them a picture and they understand how to add connections that can help them reduce costs or increase revenue. Equinix's established existing customer network is our secret sauce.

(Note: Figure 12.1 depicts a healthy data center ecosystem, which is characterized by a wide variety of firm types. This mixture can broaden a firm's reach and from the standpoint of a data center provider, diversifies our business.)

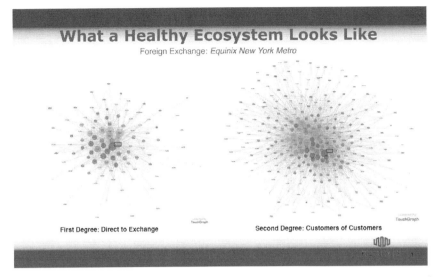

Foreign Exchange: *Equinix New York Metro*

First Degree: Direct to Exchange   Second Degree: Customers of Customers

FIGURE 12.1   Reprinted with permission of Equinix.

Can you discuss data center usage by asset class and which asset classes are at the forefront?

Foreign exchange markets were the first to democratize data center access because foreign exchange [FX] trading venues decided against creating their own proprietary data centers. FX venues were the first movers into data centers and, as a result of their customer base, pulled through dozens and dozens of very active trading firms. As the data center model proved itself to be effective and efficient, data center customers grew their presences. Equinix data center facilities in New York host nine different currency trading venues.

It seems counterintuitive, but in those early days competing FX venues became our customers as well. Usually customers want to differentiate themselves. We believe that part of our appeal was and continues to be that Equinix is not an exchange or network or financial extranet, or even a market data company. We were and remain a pure play data center model. Equinix as a company did not originate in the financial services industry, though now the financial industry [is] our biggest growing segment and one that the company highlights in earnings calls.

Our financial services segment does over USD 300 million in annual revenue.

How are global data centers keeping pace with capacity demands?

Building physical data centers is very capital intensive. New data centers can cost upwards of USD 200–300 million. It requires a great deal of fiscal discipline for a company to be able to build ahead of demand. Equinix data centers are growing in all global financial centers, which also happen to be the most expensive real estate markets in the world. We have a global footprint of 105 data centers in 38 markets in 13 countries and cover the world's top 16 financial centers. Those numbers continue to grow. Equinix is building ahead of demand in the most expensive markets in the world: Tokyo, New York City, London. Our competition cannot afford to build ahead in all of these cities. Our strong fiscal situation, and the advance capacity planning that it permits, differentiates us.

What are the latest technologies that you are implementing?

This admission may surprise some readers: Our technology is simple. Equinix made a conscious decision not to implement the most advanced technologies. We liken our role to the operator in the old switchboard model. Our business is to provide layer one, or physical, connections. We avoid introducing technology where it is not needed in order to reduce complexity. This strategy offers many benefits for customers in terms of security, costs, [and so forth]. "Back to simple" is our motto.

If you connect customers through a switch platform (which we do not do) there is a danger of that platform being hacked or someone fat fingering a command and taking a switch down. Our goal is to alleviate customer concerns with regard to uptime. When customers come into one of our datacenters and see our physical model, they immediately recognize the value in its simplicity.

The fact that we utilize simple technology does not mean that we are not innovating in other areas. We have invested a great deal in the efficient utilization of power. For example, our Amsterdam data center is cooled using cold water. Those advances are positive for Equinix and our customers on the cost side and reduce our carbon footprint.

From the data center provider side, what are the technological challenges associated with serving financial market participants?

The financial markets have a unique problem of throughput, which many market participants fail to recognize because they focus on either lower-latency or higher bandwidth. The Flash Crash was a crisis of throughput because so much information was flowing between so many different places. They look to implement fatter or shorter pipes, but it is a combination of the two that solves many performance problems. Data centers solve those challenges. In a data center environment, it is possible for customers to immediately increase throughput by five times the bandwidth from 5,000 or 10,000 to 40,000 megabits per second because their connections are hardwired.

From a technology standpoint, do the high levels of security requirements for financial services customers differ from those in other sectors? What types of new technologies are making data centers safer?

One important security consideration is uptime. Data centers in general address downtime risks. In the highly competitive trading industry, downtime risks are huge. If you are down even a few minutes, people will move away from your firm or trading venue. They may trickle back over next few days. Businesses cannot afford to get that wrong.

Certainly a lot of people move into our sites because of physical security. Our data centers feature biometric hand scanners, stringent ID requirements and video surveillance. Firms put their trust in us because of their fiduciary responsibilities. They cannot get this type of security in the back of a corporate office.

Security concerns are shared by all of our customers, across a variety of industries. Our simple model, which is providing physical connections, reduces opportunities for vulnerabilities in the chain. A great deal of innovation is occurring in the area of security software.

What new technologies from outside financial services will be the next to be adopted by data centers that serve financial services?

As a data center provider, we are in a good position to spot developing trends. We are witnessing a lot of growth in the cloud community. In fact, many customers run private clouds for either storage or computing from within our datacenters. Another trend is a steady growth in firms outsourcing their storage and computing to cloud providers within our datacenters.

What is the next trend for data centers?

One of the next big trends will be interconnecting multiple industries to add value in creative ways like in the sharing of data points on production, consumption, and other predictive numbers.

There is also a discernible trend toward convergence between mobile payments and mobile banking. Mobile network operators and financial services are natural partners. Just as there is an ecosystem in electronic trading, the same exists in mobile banking.

Can you make the case for the neutral versus the proprietary data center?

In many cases, companies need a single location where they can group technology once they have made an acquisition. Or they do not want to be dependent on a vendor. Many customers prefer the agnostic data center model.

What are the challenges of establishing a global footprint (e.g., in emerging markets)?

The challenges associated with entering new markets are impacted by the nuances of each market. For example, in Brazil it was easier for Equinix to acquire. Brazilian laws and tax structures are complicated, and it can take years to set up a commercial entity. Acquisition helped us to achieve quicker time to market. We find that to be true especially in many emerging markets. Another such situation is China, where we have five data centers in Shanghai. We are the only global data center operator with facilities in China, which certainly gives our customers a first-mover advantage.

Are you seeing migration to data centers pick up in certain geographic areas? Can you discuss?

Asia is a very high growth area in financial services and it is the highest growth market for Equinix. We are seeing more of our existing customers deploy in several different markets with us simultaneously. We focus on 16 global financial markets, and it is not uncommon for customers to enter six or eight markets with us. Part of the rationale is the standardization that our model offers. Customers recognize that they can simply replicate the setups that they already have in place at our data centers in other markets. Firms increasingly understand that it is a simple process to duplicate their data center presences in new markets because they do not have to go through a new learning process. It is turnkey.

In a telling anecdote, we just built a data center that we call Tokyo 3. The first 12 customers in that data center were all existing Equinix customers in other markets. The first 11 of those customers were not Japanese.

Can you talk about security concerns with data centers and managed services respectively?

We have multiple layers of security. Security is an important area of investment for us, especially in terms of building [structures] as well as access controls.

In addition to features like biometric scanning and strict identification policies, our data centers are blastproof and feature bulletproof walls. If anyone were able to get past our first-level security features we even have things like man traps in place, which physically trap intruders until police arrive.

Within the trade cycle, where will data centers have the biggest impact within the next several years and how?

Where we are today versus five years ago is that in those days, we offered proximity to exchange (or trading platform) matching engines and we were primarily used for trade execution. Since 2007 or 2008 market participants have been utilizing data centers to help mitigate risk in a variety of ways. Increasingly, they are using trade information to manage risk and are co-locating risk management engines as well so that risk management also benefits from reduction in latency. In today's algorithmic world, that is a must.

An important part of our business is connecting customers with information sources, which is driving our growth. The next five years will be about tackling the challenges of real-time risk analytics, counterparty, execution risk, and portfolio risk. We will also see a convergence of financial markets and cloud because much of that can be outsourced (e.g., value at risk [VAR] calculations).

Can you discuss regulatory reform and how the data center is meeting changing regulatory and compliance requirements?

Data centers provide stability and oversight. The move from OTC to swap execution facilities, and the Basel III unified regulation both will drive electronic trading to platforms. It is the biggest change over the last 20 years.

Equinix is conduit for trading. We already host many of the swap execution facilities (SEFs), global trade repositories, and several clearing platforms. Many of those affected do not like the change, but regulators have expressed a clear preference for more electronic trading, and that mandate will really change interaction [especially for those in previously non-electronic markets].

Is there concentration risk when a data center is "too popular"?

It is not our desire to host the global financial system within our data centers. We can host a matching engine or an access node, but our goal is not to do 100 percent of every customer's business. That would be physically and economically impossible for us.

For example, NYSE runs its own network and its own data center, and we provide an access node. We host many access nodes. Many of our customers maintain a couple of cabinets with us, and we believe this model is a healthy one for the overall market structure. We see our core business as specializing in creating dense interconnection points for the financial markets.

What would you say to those who would argue that the data center ecosystem is making trading too fast?

There are two sides to fast. Speed will not make a bad trade better. Speed solely for the purpose of speed does not benefit the market. It is an arms race that can bankrupt firms that try to reach zero. There are plenty of examples of that. On the other hand, firms can better mitigate risk by being quick. Technology is going to continue to make things faster.

Market participants have to dictate when and how the brakes will be applied like the proposed "half-second rule" or "time to live" for packets. If speed impacts market quality, things will change. The market will not need a regulatory push in order to prompt corrective action when market opportunities decline.

With regard to the speed issue, we are observing that many market participants are abandoning the "race to zero" and instead opting to optimize data inputs to gain an advantage in the pre-trade decision-making process. We try to promote the "trading smarter" trend by providing customers access to the vast number of information sources, including index providers and other economic sources that are also our data center customers. It is a natural area of growth for us.

What keeps you up at night?

Overregulation is probably the biggest concern because it has the potential to unleash unintended consequences. Conflicting rules internationally, transaction taxes, the "half-second rule"—they all introduce uncertainty in the markets as well as add to the cost of doing business. Layer on top of that higher clearing costs with the onset of OTC clearing, and a worrying trend is discernible. Participants are concerned about the cumulative effect of too much rule making across multiple markets and asset classes. I spend a lot of time educating regulators on the financial ecosystem and interconnectivity so that they can understand what ripple effects may happen as a result of proposed regulatory changes.

How did you help customers to keep running smoothly during the Flash Crash?

There were 2.8 million messages per second at the peak of the flash crash in U.S. options markets. The sheer volume overwhelmed the technology that was in place at the time. The Flash Crash was really a market data blackout because market participants could not get pricing information. Firms were not willing to participate because they were getting conflicting price information.

As documented in the official SEC report, the Flash Crisis was a crisis of throughput. On the contrary, when a fat finger mistake has been made, markets rebound. But when servers are offline, participants cannot get pricing, and if they cannot get reliable pricing, they will refuse to trade.

What has been your biggest challenge, and how have you grown from it as a firm?

Staying ahead of demand is something that we have invested greatly in doing. Many companies have come to us because our competitors cannot keep pace with technology requirements. Equinix's roots in Silicon Valley have meant that we have had to deal with capacity ceilings in other industries, those with considerably higher levels of data traffic.

What would you list as the most important technological achievement within the financial services industry within the last several years? How has it been a game changer?

The adoption of the Financial Information eXchange (FIX) Protocol as an industry standard has been key to driving growth in the financial industry. It has meant that firms can access increased opportunities. In a similar way, the Internet could scale because of its common protocol, HTTP. FIX is doing that in electronic trading. It is helping businesses scale.

In your opinion, what is the next "quantum leap" in technology that will revolutionize our industry?

Complex event processing (CEP) platforms will be the next leap in trading. They will revolutionize how risk management is done as soon as they can reliably take in raw unstructured data and complex algorithms can create association. CEPs will be the dominant change agent going forward.

What lessons do you have for technologists in our industry?

The most common mistake that we see is firms buying consolidated services from the "one-man band" vendor. Trying to buy bundled solutions from one vendor is inadvisable in today's markets. Specialization is the way to go because it permits firms to select the best providers for the services that they need. What's more, if firms use the same vendor as 200 of their peers, they have no competitive advantage. How you assemble your solution can give you an edge.

 ## Key Learning Points

- The chief advantage of a data center is its ability to help users save costs. Data centers offer customers the ability to quickly and cost-effectively connect across the aisle to key vendors or customers. Hosting many systems under one roof has changed the economic model and made it possible for firms to expand their networks at a reasonable cost, and at significantly reduced time to market.

- In today's world, data centers are the financial industry's electronic meeting points. In a well-populated data center, businesses can virtually meet more of their peers and develop joint opportunities for growth.

- Our business is to provide layer one, or physical, connections. We avoid introducing technology where it is not needed in order to reduce complexity. This strategy offers many benefits for customers in terms of security, costs, and so forth. "Back to simple" is our motto.

CHAPTER 13

Evolution

The New Revolution in Trading Systems Design

A s discussed in the previous chapter on data centers, the industry is more interconnected than ever before. Technology has facilitated the creation of vast networks that enable participants to operate globally, but also introduced a large number of dependencies among participants. In this chapter, the focus is on how the interdependency among market participants slows the pace of technological change. But, it makes the case that this slower pace of technological change reflects the operational realities of complex global markets. Gradual, well-executed change is not only more manageable for market participants; it also reduces risks involved in hasty implementation.

121

With few exceptions, the financial world has embraced electronic trading. Since its infancy in the 1990s, trading technology has continued to improve incrementally to provide customers with more sophisticated functionality, increased throughput, flexibility, and stability. Whereas exchanges once provided their customers with round-trip times in the seconds, now they deliver in microseconds. Commonly referred to as the "arms" race, the push to increase trading speed has been so successful that the market has now moved to tackle other challenges like the attainment of consistency in roundtrip times, handling massive amounts of market data, and applying technological advances to increase market safety, like in the development of automated risk control mechanisms.

Despite its revolutionary beginnings, electronic trading is now mainstream. And the fact that adoption of electronic trading is so widespread has impacted the way that exchanges and vendors can introduce changes in technology. Customers are connected to myriad exchange and other platforms around the world, access massive amounts of market data, and interface with hundreds of complex front-, middle-, and back-office systems. From a practical standpoint, they cannot be expected to frequently implement releases that would cause them to have to implement major changes in their in-house systems and invest considerable capital in migration processes. Logically, the introduction of new technology is slowed down by practical business concerns.

The gradual introduction of new technology and functionality lends itself to an evolutionary approach rather than revolution in the area of trading systems design. With practical concerns in mind, trading systems providers and others have opted to introduce new releases on a rolling basis, rather than follow a big bang approach. And from a business continuity standpoint, this development is net-net a positive one for the market as a whole.

■ Jürg Spillmann and Wolfgang Eholzer, Eurex Exchange

Jürg Spillmann is the deputy CEO and head of information technology and operations for Eurex Exchange and Eurex Clearing and is overall responsible for technology. His colleague Wolfgang Eholzer is head of trading systems design for the exchange.

From 1988 to 1995, Jürg served as chief information officer of SOFFEX. He served as general manager of Eurex Frankfurt AG. Mr. Spillmann played an instrumental role in the development of the fully electronic trading system that represents the centerpiece of today's SWX Swiss Exchange. Mr. Spillmann has been deputy chairman of Eurex since 1997. He serves as director of Eurex Clearing AG and Eurex Zurich AG. He has been a director of International Securities Exchange Holdings, Inc. since December 19, 2007. Mr. Spillmann served as chief information officer of SIX Swiss Exchange Ltd. (also known as SWX Swiss Exchange) since 1995. He has been chairman of the Group Executive Committee of Swx Group since October 2002. He serves as chairman of the Group Executive Committee of SIX Group Ltd. (formerly Swiss Financial Market Services AG). Mr. Spillmann completed his studies in mathematics at the ETH Zurich in 1978.

Wolfgang is Eurex's head of trading system design. Since 2007 he has been in charge of the Eurex Technology Roadmap, which resulted in the delivery of the high-speed trading interfaces for order handling and market data. In addition, he is responsible for performance monitoring and capacity planning, as well as for the implementation of the new trading architecture Eurex has introduced at the end of 2012. He is also in charge of new trading functionality and has a particular focus on achieving low latency and high throughput. Prior to his work at Eurex, Wolfgang was in charge of application development for the electronic trading systems Eurex and Xetra at Deutsche Börse Systems, the IT subsidiary of Deutsche Börse Group. Before joining Deutsche Börse Systems, Wolfgang spent two and a half years with Cambridge University (UK) as a research associate in applied mathematics and theoretical physics.

In addition to their line responsibilities, together the team is responsible for the recent introduction of a completely new trading architecture for Eurex Exchange. The new system represents a complete overhaul of the Eurex® system, which has been in place since the early 1990s. In this interview, the pair discusses the evolutionary nature of their new architecture, the challenges posed by implementing greenfield technology, and their views on technological innovation in financial services.

Is evolution the new revolution in trading systems design?

When trading became electronic, that was revolutionary. But large-scale changes like that happen very infrequently in most industries. When we launched electronic trading in the 1990s, we changed the game. Since then, ourselves included, change has been incremental. And in many ways, that is a very positive development for the industry. You cannot have revolutionary changes every year and expect the market to keep up. Our goal is a continuum.

Change will still happen—big change. In a simple example, some pits are still open outcry. Will the transition to electronic trading for them be revolutionary? In the true sense of the word, it will not be. But you can believe that for those traders, it will represent a sea change.

You cannot have revolutionary changes every year and expect the market to keep up. Our goal is a continuum.

In the absence of revolution, can innovation still occur? What kind of changes can we expect going forward?

Innovation is a risk-bearing undertaking and larger, especially public, companies have problems with the approach more generally. There is simply more at risk. Shareholders restrict the ability to invest in experimental technologies.

When we look at our industry, trading firms are nimble and very innovative. And that innovation is rewarded. As a partner to them, we benefit from their experience as a group in that many of them are intimately involved in our design specifications and testing.

We think that our approach in the development of our new trading architecture has been a success in allowing our staff to innovate in the design of certain elements. Our new system looks roughly the same to the market, provides similar functionality, [and so forth], but we allowed for creativity when designing the "guts." We dared to change certain things, to push the envelope.

What do you believe is your biggest technological achievement, and how has it affected your firm?

Without a doubt the launch of our Technology Roadmap has been a key achievement on the technology side. This roadmap was a plan that we released early to the market to show how we would implement incremental change in our system over time in order to meet market needs. It included a menu of connectivity alternatives for different customer types, including but certainly not limited to high-frequency trading (HFT) firms.

The initial, one-size-fits all approach was just not working anymore. To meet this reality head on, we developed a component approach to delivering market needs. Connectivity, or how customers access markets, is arguably the most involved and complicated component of participation in global electronic markets. Undeniably, the high-frequency interfaces offered by exchanges and other trading systems providers have met with widespread adoption by a large percentage of their important high-volume customer bases. However, for a large percentage of participants that employ non-latency-sensitive trading and investment strategies, high-frequency connectivity is technology overkill. In addition, this ultra-fast connectivity comes with a price tag that some market participants find hard to swallow. With an eye toward diversification, we have recognized the need to offer a menu of connectivity alternatives that fit the needs of a wider audience.

Remember at that time we were dealing with a mature, older system. Yet we found a way. The introduction of our new system has been easier, in a way, as it is greenfield.

How has your recent technology directly impacted the market?

Our levels of transparency set a new standard within the marketplace. So, in a sense it is that we talk openly about our technology. We provide a wide range of statistics and have built in measuring points within the system to allow others to independently verify.

The new trading architecture that we introduced at Eurex Exchange in 2012 will raise expectations in terms of consistency in roundtrip times.

(Note: Figure 13.1 illustrates the reduction on round-trip times prior to the introduction of Eurex Exchange's new trading architecture.)

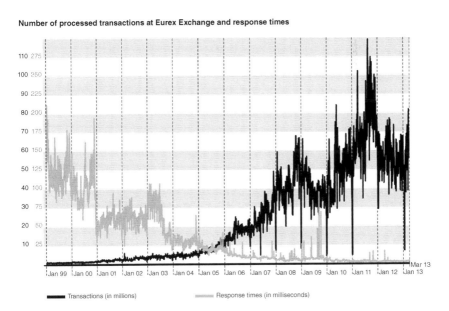

Number of processed transactions at Eurex Exchange and response times

Transactions (in millions)   Response times (in milliseconds)

FIGURE 13.1   Reprinted with permission of Eurex Exchange.

In the development of trading systems, is it a one-way street? To what extent do user demands rein in the development process?

Users tend to demand what they see from the outside, and focus on functionality and interfaces, as they should. We are proponents of a collaborative approach in the development process, and we certainly make our own internal decisions with regards to operating systems, hardware, [and so forth].

What keeps you up at night?

In launching a product as large as a completely new trading architecture we asked ourselves, "Did we overlook something fundamental?" Ours was a greenfield approach, so you ask yourself, "Can we carry it on in the second or third releases?"

From a project management standpoint, "Did we get everything?" Cores are the easiest to integrate. It is the interfacing with 500 different systems that needed to be done both on our side and the member side. Another concern is, though our customers provided significant input and were involved in testing, "Did we omit something fundamental, and if we have to add it, will it break our design principles?"

How do you balance the needs of different participant types when developing a system?

Of course firms have also driven development of our technology. Some 90 percent of all orders and quotes are entered into our system using our high-frequency interfaces.

(Note: Figure 13.2 illustrates the growth in utilization of the Eurex Enhanced Transaction Solution high-frequency interface.)

Conversely, their existence has also encouraged us to develop separate solutions for important non-latency-sensitive customers. For example, we invest in functionality that may be beneficial for non-algo firms. It is in our fundamental interest to support our diversified customer base.

Interestingly, the algo solutions that we provide are adopted by the lion's share of the market. It is our experience that trading firms self-select into the high-frequency group. It is the old "I am responsible for 25 percent of the overall daily volume in x product." But there certainly are a lot of firms

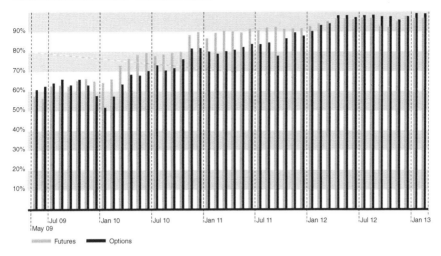

Enhanced Transaction Solution – transactions entered

Futures   Options

FIGURE 13.2   Reprinted with permission of Eurex Exchange.

that claim that. Many customers simply think that they need a Porsche to keep pace. Choosing connectivity is a cost issue for many firms, and our solutions provide flexibility. Before, in terms of technology, we made participants "lock in" a solution.

How are you implementing IT innovations from the broader industry? Do you actively seek out non-financial industry sources?

We adopt technology from the broader industry as we need it. In what we call time-based decisions, we pick the best, most appropriate technology for our purposes.

Working with select software vendors over a time period leads to the development of trusted relationships with providers, and in some cases, we are trial customers for new technologies. A good example of our willingness to adopt new technology is our use of Infiniband for our core network.

What trends are you following in the area of coding?

With our new trading architecture specifically, we are a lot more diverse in coding. Different parts of the new architecture have different needs, and so we use different coding languages. In fact, we think that using more heterogeneous base elements (different coding languages, network techniques, etc.) has increased our productivity. From our history using mainly C and COBOL under OpenVMS as well as Ethernet, this was a big step. We had to redevelop the whole design process.

Do universities or research facilities play a role in your development process? If yes, how?

We support universities broadly and involve ourselves in projects at a number of universities on the technology side as interesting and relevant topics arise. As a company, we benefit from the European educational system that requires a corporate sponsor for many PhD students writing their theses. In addition, the European apprenticeship model requires on-the-job learning, and we employ a large number on the technology side.

What are your views on the arms race (speed versus functionality)?

We have to offer both. In terms of functionality, we ask ourselves whether we need to fragment things [markets] on purpose. We like central order books, but is there a case where it makes sense to offer different compartments to different market participants? Another consideration that we have to weigh is whether certain functionality is worth it in terms of a cost/benefit ratio. Finally, catering to the needs of both latency-sensitive and those with other types of trading strategies helps us diversify our business.

How do you attract and, importantly, retain the best talent in such a competitive industry?

Working on one of the world's most prominent trading and clearing systems is an exciting prospect for many. We think like a small company when it comes to technology and encourage independent thinking and experimentation, which technologists value in an employer.

In fact, the longevity of our technologists is extremely high, which has allowed us to build a stable of experts. And on the career development side, those [who] opt to leave have valuable experience that customers are willing to pay for.

Are IT professionals in our industry the new physicians, and can you discuss the around-the-clock demands on your schedules?

As a company we follow an around-the-clock service model and provide support from Europe and the [United States]. That helps us spread out the load—and catch some thieves! True story: One of our network staff in Chicago was monitoring customer connections during the European night hours when a given European customer's server connections dropped off one by one. He called the local European IT contact, woke him up, and raised the alarm. His European IT contact got dressed, went down to the office, and interrupted the robbery of his firm! Maybe we are the new police officers?

What do you view to be the biggest impacts of global regulatory reform on IT?

In terms of IT, regulatory reform will have a number of impacts, several of which are especially important for an exchange and clearinghouse: Data storage for compliance will entail creative database and retrieval solutions.

Can you discuss how regional issues or concerns affect your designs?

Decentralization has been our mantra from the get-go and made us think globally much earlier than the competition. Our global outlook has impacted the way we have designed our system (e.g., the placement of access points in global financial centers). With the advances in telecommunications networks over the past decade, regional issues are less of a concern on the technology side and more a business issue (for example, trading hours or matching engines in different time zones).

In your opinion, what is the next "quantum leap" in trading technology that will revolutionize our industry?

We foresee a number of changes that will change user behavior and continue to accelerate processing speed. When it comes to behavioral changes in the financial markets, the tablet will be a game changer. As soon as mobile instruments become more powerful and flexible, they will further decentralize markets. Since our industry requires such high levels of security, once those levels can be guaranteed to individual users mobility will increase dramatically.

Another very promising area is the use of field programmable gate arrays (FPGAs) and graphical processing units (GPUs), which speed up processing across a variety of areas. If cloud computing can ever deliver on its promises, it would bring significant efficiencies to the market. At the current moment we are far away from those promises. Rules, especially on compliance side, will also have to keep up.

These forecasts go back to our theme. We are looking at a series of evolutionary changes that improve on existing behaviors and processes, and not a revolution per se.

 Key Learning Points

- Innovation is a risk-bearing undertaking and larger, especially public, companies have problems with the approach more generally. There is simply more at risk. Shareholders restrict the ability to invest in experimental technologies.

- The initial one-size-fits-all approach was just not working anymore. To meet this reality head on, we developed a component approach to delivering market needs. Ultra-fast connectivity comes with a price tag that some market participants find hard to swallow. With an eye toward diversification, we have recognized the need to offer a menu of connectivity alternatives that fit the needs of a wider audience.

- Interestingly, the algo solutions that we provide are adopted by the lion's share of the market. It is our experience that trading firms self-select into the high-frequency group.

EVOLUTION

CHAPTER 14

FIX

The Power of Standardization

As the Financial Information eXchange electronic communications protocol (FIX Protocol) gains further traction in a greater number of asset classes, it brings with it significant synergies for certain types of less-latency-sensitive market participants. In this chapter, W. Brennan Carley of Thomson Reuters explains how global standards continue to drive synergies. The widespread adoption of FIX enabled not only the rapid expansion of electronic markets but also played an important role in leveling the playing field among brokerage firms, exchanges, and electronic communication networks (ECNs), making it possible for firms to compete on price, execution quality, and other value-add services. Although the FIX protocol dates from the 1990s, its impact is not a thing of the past.

Going forward, FIX will continue to democratize new markets. In addition to its expansion into different asset classes like the OTC markets, FIX has the potential to streamline post-trade processes. As regulatory oversight imposes additional compliance demands, FIX will assume additional importance there as well. Finally, perhaps the crowning achievement of FIX is that it proves that the industry can work together cooperatively to deliver synergies and in doing so, provides a model for future joint development work.

The story of the widely accepted FIX protocol and how it came into being is unique. Standards are rare in financial services technology, especially in this highly proprietary industry. In general, developing and implementing standards entails a great deal of effort, work that does not positively impact a company's profitability. Plus, with such a large and varied group of participants, it is a difficult process to develop universally accepted stand-ards in any area, let alone in the complex and highly customized are of in-formation technology. Given this background, the achievements of FIX are even more impressive.

■ W. Brennan Carley, Thomson Reuters

Brennan Carley is global head of the Elektron Transactions and Enterprise Platform businesses at Thomson Reuters. As head of Elektron Transactions, he leads the firms business in electronic trading in equities and other listed securities, including FIX order routing and indications of interest. As head of Enterprise Platform, Brennan leads the Thomson Reuters' core data plat-form business that allows financial professionals to control information flow by connecting all of the different applications needed for trading, invest-ment, risk management, and compliance.

Brennan joins Thomson Reuters from Proton Advisors and brings almost 30 years of experience in trading technology and trading communications. As founder and managing principle of Proton Advisors, Brennan provid-ed advisory services to private equity funds, venture investors, and their portfolio companies in trading technology and telecommunications. As a consultant through Proton Advisors, Brennan served as SVP of product marketing at Spread Networks, a provider of ultra-low-latency connectivity to the financial markets.

He previously was COO of NYFIX (now NYSE Technologies), was CTO and founder of financial extranet BT Radianz, and was head of technology for Instinet. He has been a director on the boards of companies including Marketcetera and Yipes, and is an adjunct professor of business and technol-ogy management at New York University.

Brennan earned a bachelor of arts degree in economics from New York University and has done graduate studies at Columbia University, Harvard Business School, and Massachusetts Institute of Technology.

How has the FIX protocol impacted the industry to date?

The FIX protocol has done nothing less than revolutionize trading and re-shape the entire trading ecosystem. While electronic trading would have happened without FIX (and some electronic trading preceded FIX), the rate at which the equities markets have converted to electronic trading would never have been achieved without FIX. This has lowered the cost of trading, enabled entirely new trading strategies, and has accelerated the shift in power in the industry to the buy-side.

What prompted so many profit-driven entities to work together to establish an industry standard?

When FIX was first developed (by Salomon Brothers and Fidelity investments), it did not initially appear to be a foregone conclusion that FIX would gain widespread adoption. There were a number of proprietary protocols in use at the time, some developed by brokers and some developed by stock exchanges. Many of those exchanges and brokers (including Instinet, where I worked at the time) would have preferred to keep their proprietary protocols; they were up and running, and once a customer had programmed to them, they were less likely to switch. So brokers and exchanges with existing protocols had a lot of reasons to resist FIX. But the industry quickly embraced FIX for three reasons.

Electronic trading was still in its infancy when FIX was developed. While screen-based trading had been around for a while, the idea of programmatic trading (i.e., machine to machine communications) was still very new, and the use of an order management system (OMS) or execution management system (EMS) was also quite new. These things needed message-based communications protocols, and FIX came along before any other protocol was well established. Even though several exchanges and brokers had proprietary protocols, the use of these protocols was very limited and the market was fragmented. No one protocol was dominant. So FIX was not trying to displace an entrenched proprietary standard, it was trying to displace a babble of protocols. Probably the most important was that customers, the buy-side, wanted it. Sophisticated buy-side firms like Twentieth Century (now American Century) and Fidelity told their brokers that they wanted to use FIX. While exchanges and brokers might have preferred to continue using their own homegrown protocols, it really was inevitable that an open, customer-supported protocol would displace a bunch of proprietary protocols, none of which was very well entrenched or dominant. Ironically, the initial adoption of FIX was the asset management and the brokerage community, both profit-driven entities, and the last adopters were the exchanges and clearing houses, which at that time were mutually owned non-profit industry utilities.

How has the increase in standardization that FIX has achieved helped to level the playing field in financial services?

By establishing an easily implemented open standard, FIX has not completely leveled the playing field; brokers, ECNs, alternative trading systems (ATSs), exchanges, and multilateral trading facilities (MTFs) in Europe have many opportunities to differentiate their execution services. But FIX has eliminated differentiation based on communications technology, and indirectly based on trading front ends (EMSs and OMSs). Asset managers and hedge funds can use virtually any EMS or OMS to trade with just about any broker, ECN, or exchange. The technical barrier has been lowered by FIX, and it has become much easier for the buy side to switch from one broker to another. The FIX protocol has standardized messaging formats, and FIX networks have made the physical connectivity to many destinations easier and more cost effective. This has allowed electronic trading to become much more friction free, reducing cost, and allowing brokers and ECNs to compete on the basis of execution quality, market impact, and other services.

In what ways have global standards like FIX enhanced profitability for those that adopt them?

FIX has created whole new businesses and enhanced profitability for some participants, while driving down profitability for others. For the buy side, FIX has reduced the cost of trading and created greater competition for their order flow. It has enabled enhanced transparency of execution costs, which has contributed to declining costs of execution.

FIX has enabled the creation of FIX-based businesses, ranging from OMS and EMS platforms to FIX routing networks. Other businesses have sprung up to provide tools for trading, based on FIX. And of course FIX has made it possible for alternate trading venues (ECNs, ATSs, MTFs) to be established and attract liquidity.

While FIX has reduced cost and improved profitability for the buy side and created a whole industry, like any disruptive technology it has contributed to decreasing revenues for brokers and exchanges in the face of intensified competition. Some of those have thrived by driving down their costs; others have suffered with high cost bases and decreased profitability.

Is standardization a good thing, or is FIX adoption eliminating a technology edge for those that adopt it?

On the one hand, standardization reduces the opportunity for innovation of the thing being standardized. By standardizing a single trade communications format, it is much harder for any firm to offer new innovations in trade messaging. It also slows industry innovation in trade messaging, because it requires some level of consensus and cooperation. Imagine if Apple had to go to a committee every time it wanted to offer a new feature.

On the other hand, standardization accelerates innovation in two ways. It allows innovation to occur within the context of FIX (i.e., FIX Protocol Limited [FPL]). Once an innovative development is agreed upon, the adoption of that innovation can occur much more quickly. So the development of innovative technology may be slower, but the dispersion of that innovation into the market can be much quicker. Then, by standardizing messaging, the industry has been able to shift its resources from developing "yet another messaging protocol" onto more useful forms of innovation that build on top of FIX.

What other standards are out there in financial services? What are their strengths versus FIX?

While there are battling standards for things like symbology and XML-based standards for electronic documents (e.g., XBRL), in the area of messaging standards the main ones besides FIX are ISO 20022, SWIFT, and FpML. FpML is optimized for over-the-counter (OTC) derivatives, where deal structures and trading workflows are much more complex than for instruments traded on-exchange.

SWIFT has developed several messaging standards over the years, and focuses primarily in inter-bank payments messaging, and more recently on post-trade messaging in securities.

ISO 20022 is really an umbrella standard that allows messages to be described in a standard way. Current versions of FIX, FpML, and SWIFT messages are all described using ISO 20022, and all of these organizations work together.

In what ways is FIX continuing to promote the globalization of financial markets?

While FIX started as a U.S.–centric cash equities protocol, it quickly evolved to embrace global markets and other asset classes including FX (foreign exchange) and fixed income. Customers can connect to global FIX networks that enable them to establish their presences around the world. This makes it possible for a U.S. asset manager to connect its OMS to a broker in Brazil, or a hedge fund in Hong Kong to connect to a broker in London, just as easily as it is to connect to a domestic broker. In practice, of course, while FIX solves the connectivity problem, brokers and buy sides must still establish credit arrangements, clearing and settlement, [and so forth]. And while a broker in Tokyo can use FIX to connect to an ECN in New York, all of the commercial arrangements must still be in place.

Until recently, this has meant that global trading took place by using global banks. The hedge fund in Hong Kong would trade with the Hong Kong office of a global bank that had a brokerage license and exchange membership in London. Following the financial crisis, however, many banks with global ambition have consolidated their operations and focused on their home markets. French banks with formerly global ambition have slimmed down their Americas and Asian operations and focus now on the Eurozone. Japanese banks have done the same with their European and Americas operations. A model that is re-emerging is one in which brokers in one country have relationships with friendly brokers in another country. So the hedge fund in Hong Kong might have a (FIX-enabled) local relationship with a broker in Hong Kong that routes the order (via FIX) to a UK bank that, in turn, routes the order (via FIX) to market in London. The standardization on a single protocol makes it easier for cross-border activity to take place, even as market structure continues to evolve.

Are certain types of market participants more readily adopting FIX, and for which applications?

Within the cash equities market, FIX adoption is pervasive across all market participants. It began with participants who were either large enough to have sophisticated in-house order management and trading systems, or who had systematic trading strategies (e.g., pairs trading, statistical arbitrage) and the brokers who facilitated those customers. It spread from there, and is now widely adopted by all but the smallest firms (e.g., those who outsource their trading.)

As FIX is being adopted in FX and in fixed income, it is following the same trajectory as it did in equities, but with an accelerator: Firms that have already implemented FIX for their equity trading, especially those who have cross-asset trading strategies, have been among the first to adopt FIX for FX and fixed income by leveraging their existing systems and skills.

As FIX is being adopted in FX and in fixed income, it is following the same trajectory as it did in equities, but with an accelerator.

Over the next few years, I expect that FIX will be broadly used across all exchange-based (or "exchange-like"; e.g., swap execution facilities (SEFs) and organized trading facilities) asset classes, a category that will expand as regulatory forces push more trading onto an exchange-like model.

FIX started in the [United States], but is now truly global, with leadership coming from all areas of the globe. FPL, the governing body for FIX, has active development taking place from participants in Europe, Asia, Latin America, and the United States.

Is FIX relevant only for non-latency-sensitive applications?

FIX is the protocol of choice for all but the most latency-sensitive trading. For firms that are pursuing purely latency-based trading strategies, or where low latency is a substantial element of their alpha capture, exchange proprietary and binary protocols are generally used. While this kind of trading has had high visibility in the press and accounts for a substantial portion of daily volume, the number of participants who engage in these strategies is fairly small (around 40–50 globally), and they tend not to use standard software or protocols of any kind. They are like the Formula 1 racecar drivers, happy to trade off cost-effective and standard systems in return for a few microseconds of performance advantage.

How important is FIX in execution? Is it more or less important in other areas of the trade cycle?

FIX has had the most impact on the pre-trade through trade stages of the trade cycle, which makes sense when one considers that the post-trade world was (and remains) very centralized and standardized around a small number of industry utilities (e.g., Central Securities Depositories).

FIX has made some inroads into the post-trade market, in particular in the area of trade allocations, and I expect that this will continue to grow as it is a natural extension of the existing FIX-based workflow.

FIX has had the most impact in order routing, initially in cash and block trading, and more recently in algorithmic and systematic trading—delivery of orders from buy-side firms to brokers. With our current fragmented market structure, institutions have increased demand to get trades done in block size, and I expect that FIX-based messaging will have a growing impact on the block trading world, primarily in the form of indications of interest.

Will FIX ever replace proprietary interfaces?

Where proprietary interfaces are not dominant or where there are multiple proprietary interfaces to choose from, FIX has an opportunity to grow and replace such interfaces. But where there are well-established proprietary interfaces, there is little opportunity (or advantage) for the industry to switch from those to FIX, at least not in the near term.

Is the preference for proprietary versus FIX of a technical or bureaucratic nature? How can it be overcome?

The choice of FIX versus proprietary standards is really driven by two things. In the case of the ultra-low-latency community, proprietary protocols are chosen for pure performance reasons. In other areas, the primary drivers are market factors; [that is] in segments of the market where there a small number of dominant players (such as central securities depositories (CSDs) or some of the derivatives exchanges) with established proprietary protocols, the market will use those protocols. In areas of the market where there are many competitors, competitive intensity is high, and barriers to entry are low, FIX is a much more attractive standard.

Are there any areas where FIX is not used today where it could lead to significant synergies?

The primary area where FIX is not used extensively today, and which could benefit from greater FIX adoption is post-trade, which would allow greater reuse of FIX-based systems/technologies, and end-to-end processing of messages. Given the number of well-established protocols in this area by dominant CSDs and other industry utilities, it seems unlikely that we will see substantial post-trade adoption of FIX in the near term.

How is FIX assisting in risk management?

FIX (and FPL) helps with risk management in three ways. First, the adoption of FIX as a standard trade messaging protocol has made it easier for firms to build risk management systems. Second, FPL has defined a set of industry best practices for pre-trade risk checks, which of course can be implemented by systems that intercept FIX-based trading messages. Of course, these same best practices can also be used on proprietary messaging interfaces as well. Finally, FIX is also being used as a messaging protocol to provide reporting to regulators.

With an eye toward regulatory developments, from a technology standpoint how can FIX assist regulators?

Regulators are struggling to catch up with the explosion in trading volumes and order volumes, and need visibility of trade messages to better understand and surveil (both in real time and afterward) financial markets. Adoption of FIX messaging has helped regulators to perform this function.

Does FIX have a place in OTC trading and clearing?

As instruments that have traditionally been traded OTC become more electronic and shift to an exchange-like model, FIX will be used as a standard messaging protocol. FIX already has functionality for trading OTC instruments, and FPL is working with ISDA (International Swaps and Derivatives Association) to develop best practices for trading interest rate swaps and credit default swaps using a combination of FIX and FpML. On the clearing side, for example, FIX 5.0 supports messages for standardized credit default swaps for clearing. A number of derivative clearing houses are using FIXML today for post-trade messaging for clearing listed derivatives, and many are adopting these systems to provide OTC derivative clearing as well.

Does the cooperative nature of FIX hinder development?

While the cooperative nature of development leads to slower development of new technologies, it has some significant benefits. It leads to more robust standards, because more participants have had the opportunity to validate the technology. Plus, the industry has greater buy-in to the technology because it has been developed in a cooperative manner. Once defined, the rate of adoption can be greater.

What would you list as the most important technological achievement within the financial services industry within the last several years? How has it been a game changer?

The single biggest technological achievement in the financial services industry has been the automation of the trade execution function. While electronic trading is not without its flaws, and the markets have seen vulnerabilities such as the Flash Crash, it is easy to forget what the markets were like before the introduction of automation. Trading costs were higher, as measured in commissions, in spread, and in market impact. Markets were less liquid, and it took more time and money to get trades done in thinly traded securities. And the markets were more opaque and more vulnerable to conflicts of interest and rigging of prices. While not perfect, electronic trading has reduced costs for investors; made it easier, more reliable, and more transparent to trade; and has enabled new kinds of investments altogether (such as exchange traded funds [ETFs], which have reduced the cost for investors to get exposure to broad segments of the market).

In your opinion, what is the next "quantum leap" in trading technology that will revolutionize our industry?

I can't predict the next "quantum leap" in trading technology for three reasons. First, we are operating in an environment that is characterized primarily by greater regulatory focus and increased pressure on costs. Most of the focus of the industry is therefore concentrated on cost reduction, standardization, and consolidation of functions (e.g., into shared utilities, whether for-profit or non-profit.) In the [United States], the financial sector's share of GDP has grown over the last 60 years from 2 percent to over 8 percent, a growth rate that is clearly not sustainable, which is one reason we are seeing consolidation of the financial sector today. Technologies like FIX are valuable tools to create efficiencies, so I am optimistic about the continued growth of FIX. But it is hard to see something that will revolutionize the industry.

As tempting as it is to look for revolutionary technologies, most technologies are incremental improvements on what was there. FIX was an evolution of earlier trade messaging protocols (at least in concept, if not in the precise syntax). Over the next few years, I expect most technology development in trading will be evolutionary, and a lot of it will be adopting and extending existing technology (including FIX) into areas that are today less automated.

Finally, as the physicist Nils Bohr (who received the Nobel Prize for his work on quantum physics, so who knows something about quantum leaps) said, "Prediction is very difficult, especially about the future." So everything I just said could be totally wrong.

What lessons do you have for technologists in our industry?

While it is important to get the technology right, technology rarely succeeds or fails based solely on the technology. Understanding the market that you operate in is critical to the success of any technology. Betamax was arguably a "better" technology than VHS, but VHS ultimately won. It won because it had a longer recording time and was more readily licensed, which led to greater availability of content. And content drove the success of VHS players. Ultimately any technology needs to succeed in the marketplace, and good technology is only one variable. FIX succeeded not because it was better than alternate technologies, but because it made it easier for buy-side institutions to build one system to connect to multiple brokers, which lowered their costs. And in that market, the bargaining power of the buy side was and remains greater than the bargaining power of the sell side. To really understand these dynamics, I would encourage any technologist to read Michael Porter (Harvard Business School), and in particular study Porter's "Five Forces" model.

Key Learning Points

■ By establishing an easily implemented open standard, FIX has not completely leveled the playing field; brokers, ECNs, ATSs, exchanges, and MTFs in Europe have many opportunities to differentiate their execution services. But FIX has eliminated differentiation based on communications technology, and indirectly based on trading front ends (EMSs and OMSs).

- The adoption of FIX as a standard trade messaging protocol has made it easier for firms to build risk management systems. FPL has defined a set of industry best practices for pre-trade risk checks, which can be implemented by systems that intercept FIX-based trading messages.

- As instruments that have traditionally been traded OTC become more electronic and shift to an exchange-like model, FIX will be used as a standard messaging protocol. FIX already has functionality for trading OTC instruments, and FPL is working with ISDA to develop best practices for trading interest rate swaps and credit default swaps using a combination of FIX and FpML.

CHAPTER 15

Big Data, Big Opportunities

In this chapter, David Siegel, Alan Choyna, and Clara Bonaccorsi of Bottom Line Metrics discuss the challenges posed by Big Data and how firms are using data to gain an edge in a variety of ways, such as the possibility to engage in more targeted marketing, better track customer behavior, recognize patterns, determine correlations between new data sets, and even perform superior business analytics. Across a variety of applications, insightful analysis of data is helping firms create an improved context for their decision-making. And putting data in the context of business challenges is a key determinant in how successful companies are in exploiting data.[*]

Arguably, financial market participants should be at an advantage in terms of data analysis, as deriving value from data has long been an important determinant of success in trading and investment. While massive amounts of data certainly are not unique to financial markets, the typical number of systems to which market participants connect complicates the problem of data management.

Big Data is a buzzword, but it refers to a very real challenge shared across industries. Today, people and systems produce more data than ever before. A report on Big Data by CRC cites various sources that predict that some customers will be storing multiple petabytes of data by 2020.[†] While some data is structured, much of the new data that is generated, like social media

---

[*] www.sas.com/resources/asset/EIU_SAS_BigData_120822.pdf.

[†] www.csc.com/insights/flxwd/78931-big_data_growth_just_beginning_to_explode.

data, falls into the unstructured category, which means that it is not well suited to relational databases, which traditionally have been used to manage data. As a result, firms are struggling with how to collect, store, and, most importantly, extract value from massive quantities of data. Despite the challenges of Big Data, its efficient utilization by firms can deliver great opportunities. Going forward, data and the information that it contains represent an especially important source of competitive advantage, especially since other technology-derived edges are increasingly short-lived.

■ David Siegel, Alan Choyna, and Clara Bonaccorsi, Bottom Line Metrics

Dave Siegel is the chief executive officer of Bottom Line Metrics (BLM), a firm that specializes in clearing data normalization and value add analysis tools. BLM's founder, original system architect, and developer, Mr. Siegel has over 20 years' experience working with high-volume, high-profile companies in the financial and trading/brokerage sectors. Prior to founding BLM, Mr. Siegel was the managing partner of Siegel Data Management, a business-consulting firm whose clients included The Northern Trust Company, ABN-AMRO, Citadel Investment Group, the Blue Cross Blue Shield Association, Man Financial Group, and REFCO Securities, and specialized trading firms such as Stafford Trading, Breakwater Trading, and Endeavor Trading.

Alan Choyna is chief technology officer of Bottom Line Metrics. He has 25 years of experience in application development and infrastructure architecture across three continents, including 17 years specifically in the financial industry. For the 12 years prior to joining BLM, Mr. Choyna was partner and CTO at Pathfinder Development, a boutique software development firm working with startup companies as well as Fortune 2000 companies such as Goldman Sachs, The Marmon Group, Mesirow Financial, Bank One, General Electric, and the *Chicago Sun-Times* media group. Prior to Pathfinder, Mr. Choyna provided software development and application architecture services to top-tier international banks including ANZ, Westpac, Banco De La Nacion, Comerica, and First Chicago/Bank One, integrating the banks' software applications with their back-office accounting systems.

Clara Bonaccorsi is product manager at Bottom Line Metrics. She brings to BLM 20 years of experience in the financial industry in the areas of clearing operations, software development and quality assurance (QA), implementation project planning cycles, and analysis of data leveraging opportunities for hedge funds, (CTAs), commodity pools, funds of funds, and proprietary trading firms. As regional operations AVP for Refco Inc., a leading futures clearing merchant (FCM), she gained experience overseeing and engaging in the daily clearing cycle, which includes customer service, balancing, deliveries, option expiration, out-trades, system testing, firm acquisition integration, data processing, and technology integration. Clara was subsequently employed by LineData Services, supporting system integration for the alternative asset management division of the company.

What are the major challenges of Big Data in financial markets?

Consistency in and the reliability of data sources are chief among the Big Data challenges, regardless of industry. The financial and commodity markets lack standards: standardization of identifiers across vendors (e.g., is this data point referring to the same company across multiple inputs, and electronic data interchange [EDI] standards). Standardization of identifiers is of greater concern to financial firms, for one, because in the equities space, the ticker, name, and CUSIP change over time. Each vendor handles these periodic changes differently, which creates a very large headache for data consumers.

One reason for the lack of uniformity is that firms are not incented to create standards because doing so does not boost returns directly. A possible reason that firms have not worked either cooperatively or on an individual basis to introduce standards may be that individual firms fear that if they standardize data they would remove important differentiators between themselves and other companies, and in doing so make it easier for customers to switch providers.

Standardization is key because it lays a foundation for efficient data utilization. When standards are in place, firms can dedicate resources to the interpretation of data, which is where data can unlock potential. Unfortunately, much of the Big Data problem is grunt work, which delays using data for value-add. Mapping data from various sources to a standardized format is the biggest inhibitor to efficiency. Interpreting data is a challenge that ranks equally with mapping in terms of difficulty. In the trading sector, the standardization of instrument symbols would facilitate analysis greatly.

In what ways are financial firms deriving value from Big Data?

Big Data represents enormous potential for a broad spectrum of financial firms. For banks and other customer-driven businesses, they can custom-tailor marketing and sales messages based on customer profiles and activities. In the case of retail banks, firms can pitch credit cards and other services based on account levels, spending habits, [and so forth]. On the trading side, firms can utilize data for pattern recognition, to discover new linkages between datasets and by extension, potentially valuable correlations [among] products, markets, and even events.

However, the reality of the current situation is that firms are having varying degrees of success in terms of the value that they are deriving from data. Generally speaking, firms are more comfortable in analyzing traditional data sources, which include data vendors and newsfeeds. Social media and other unstructured data receive a lot of press but firms grapple with how to sort through massive amounts to hone in on value. Vendors that can help trading firms and other financial market participants put data into context are becoming increasingly sought after.

Are trading firms adding to the Big Data problem?

There are a couple of factors at play. First, data generation is growing in the world at large as people are utilizing technology in new ways. Facebook and Google are just two examples. Firms across industries are utilizing it to gain insights into behavior of customers, markets, [and so forth]. The principle is the same.

In trading, the trader profile and the quant profiles are converging. Increasingly, they are people who are comfortable with data and know how to approach its analysis. These people have an appetite for data and companies are delivering it. From an asset class perspective, foreign exchange and equity options are experiencing massive increases in data generation. High-frequency trading (HFT) firms are driving this growth and most of them are multi-asset class.

How does Big Data rank among firms' overall challenges?

Within the trading industry, Big Data ranks behind trading systems, network and infrastructure performance, and management in priority, but is gaining momentum as firms enhance their understanding of what data is available and how it can be applied to enhance their competitive edge in trading strategies. For those market participants whose strategies are less latency-sensitive, the insights gleaned from data may give them another way to compete: information asymmetry.

How difficult is it to get high-quality data?

Obtaining high-quality data is still extremely difficult. Data providers spend enormous sums on cleaning their data sets and there are still numerous errors. And the situation is complicated because firms often issue corrections and restatements as well. Providers treat inputs differently; therefore you could have two providers with different value and have them both be correct. For example, in the pricing world one price feed may contain after-market values or negotiated values, and another feed may not. Or, price data may be exchange specific as opposed to consolidated. On the fundamental side, you can have one database with restatements and another as reported. These issues provide just a brief overview into the complexity of financial data.

On top of concerns about quality, it is still very expensive to get good, relatively clean data. That is one reason why many firms collect and process data themselves from sources like Bloomberg or Reuters rather than buy (clean) data directly from a provider. In our area of expertise, which is clearing, obtaining third-party data is not an option. Firms can only get their end-of-day clearing data directly from their clearers. In this way, clearing firms have a captive audience.

How is technology helping to address these challenges?

Other industries have led the way in developing databases that can handle massive amounts of data. Examples of these are Amazon's Relational Data Services (MySQL, SQL Server and Oracle) and DynamoDB, Google's Big Query and Cloud SQL (MySQL), as well as NoSQL data store technologies such as Hadoop, MapReduce, and MongoDB. As an industry, we can harness those.

Around 30 enterprise and open-source ETL (extract, transform, and load) tools are popular for helping to input data into warehouses. The healthcare industry, with its HIPAA standards, is arguably the leader in dealing with this challenge. There are several out-of-the-box software solutions that attempt to help data flow seamlessly from one end to the other, but they generally fall short because they do not understand what they are processing.

In every industry, intelligent software is helping people use data to derive business benefits. For example, there are a number of data visualization tools on the market, and they are becoming increasingly adept at providing a very good quick overview of data. In the context of clearing, they could quickly indicate the current value of any unrealized gains or if an option is in-the-money.

In the highly specialized financial markets, however, technology is insufficient in and of itself. It requires guidance from humans with experience in the subject matter. At BLM, we excel in decoding data, which in many cases includes poorly or misidentified data (for example, unrealized gains that may be hiding in a field with a nondescript header or the value of an underlying instrument may be entirely absent and must be leveraged from another source and integrated into reporting).

Does too much data cloud the picture?

Yes, too much data makes it difficult to find specific points or threads of value. It is the needle in the haystack problem: The bigger the haystack, the harder it is to find the needle. When a firm approaches data, it should have a clear understanding of what questions it wants that data to answer for it. Firms must not only invest in intelligent processing of data but also in intelligent presentation of Big Data so that businesses can better see the value.

As a vendor specializing in dealing with clearing data, we put data within the context of clearing; firms want data to provide them with a better understanding of how past positions can and will affect the future in terms of allocation of capital, in which asset class under what market conditions it performs best, [how to] accurately estimate exchange, clearing and brokerage fees, and other such studies.

Can firms reduce the Big Data problem by focusing on data they need?

Honing in on certain data may seem like a pragmatic approach but it is not a farsighted one. While firms can be relatively certain what data adds value today, five years in the future, different pieces of a data set could prove invaluable. New regulation and increasing compliance standards are further reasons why, especially in finance, firms should not cull their data.

As a vendor, we cannot make value judgments on which data is valuable. Some market participants utilize information about mainstream products; others use it to identify opportunities in fringe markets.

What value are firms extracting from clearing data?

A major focus for firms should be real-time risk management and portfolio analysis, but while managing risk in real time is the clear priority, end-of-day data can give firms an important picture that most are currently not getting. For example, clearing data can allow firms to perform better execution analysis in order to identify slippage and evaluate overall quality of fills.

Different from real-time risk analytics, which are usually done in-house, end-of-day clearing data enables the business side to automate their back-office reporting and post-trade analytics, as well as run forward-looking analytics that can lead to the better allocation of resources. Examples include studies like hypothetical forecasts based on actual history, behavioral analytics on traders and trading groups, and return on capital. Each clearing firm produces end-of-day data in a distinct format. In fact, the data is so complex that many firms fail to analyze it in a systematic way at all. When firms ignore end-of-day clearing data they miss out on opportunities to derive insights into their businesses.

As longtime participants in the capital markets, we have witnessed the rise and fall of many firms. We have seen many trading firms transition from proprietorship to company to enterprise; a major determinant of their success is whether or not it is run like a business. The importance of clearing data grows over time as it permits firms to view a longer, more complete history, and provides a number of benefits. For one, the CEO and COO get more comprehensive access to critical information, which enables closer measurement of current risk [and] better estimation of projected future risk, and provid[es] accurate trader performance analytics. The benefits of the storage of clearing data extend to compliance in that the chief compliance officer then has a data warehouse to interrogate for compliance purposes. Finally, the CFO gains a mechanism to fully automate trade reconciliation (between trading platform and cleared data), and automate many critical back-office reports, general ledger updates, and responses to auditor queries, which can often go back several years.

How has your technology impacted the market?

Our complex, automated, cash-management report anticipates balances for the next 15 business days and is used to determine the interest basis on money that will need to be borrowed from a given clearing firm, among other things. This report is unique in the space, and currently is patent-pending. It is one of our key differentiators.

We were able to create this complex software by leveraging information available in recent clearing cycles, integrating select pricing information, and leaning on our collective industry knowledge. We determine how our customers' positions at multiple clearing firms will be affected by a series of anticipated events including option expirations, futures expiration, and short stocks. Our report estimates how the interest basis for borrowing will be affected by these events and ultimately allows clients to proactively reduce interest costs.

How long does an IT edge last these days?

Putting an expiration date on an edge is tough because the duration of an edge varies greatly according to what it is. Coding (non-algorithmic) is almost commoditized. Hardware and networking are ascendant.

In your opinion, what is the next "quantum leap" in technology that will revolutionize our industry?

CEP (complex event processing) engines will take real-time risk management to the next level, especially when they are fed with high-quality, clean, and normalized data.

What do you view to be the bigger impact of global regulatory reform on IT?

Government regulation will be the biggest single driver of massive increases in data gathering and storage. Regulators will need to provide concrete prescriptions on data formats as well as type and scope of the data to be gathered. Otherwise, the burden on trading firms will be far more onerous (data ETL), and the regulators will find it difficult to extract value from data, or even worse, it will be impossible for them to decode the data that firms submit.

What data sets will financial firms gather next?

Gathering and storing data to demonstrate Basel III compliance will represent a huge challenge, and it will lead to a massive increase in the amount of data that financial firms store. Basel III will require firms to gather and store data that measures capital risk inside an organization on the enterprise, bank, bank branch office, and even on the granular customer level. This new data represents massive business opportunities, especially from a marketing and sales standpoint. Data will help financial firms better understand their customers and tailor offerings for individual users to an extent that has been impossible thus far.

Banks have previously held this data at the bank level, and have realized that the Basel data requirements have provided them with a huge opportunity to use this enterprise-wide data warehouse to improve efficiency, standardization, and importantly help all level of the enterprise make better informed decisions.

Currently, many firms have their data in silos within their various business groups, and, like banks, they recognize this inefficiency. In answer, they are focusing on creating enterprise-wide data warehouses, which are far more powerful and have the added benefit that they provide all levels of an organization with higher-quality data for enhanced decision making.

What lessons do you have for technologists in our industry?

The CTO and CIO can assist businesses greatly by identifying data sources that will provide extra information that could, in turn, deliver their traders and/or algorithms a competitive advantage.

In many companies the CIO and CTO are perceptibly lower in the hierarchy than the CEO, COO, and CFO. In our opinion, this is because technologists are not as familiar with the business. To solve this problem, technologists should be more business-centric. In our space, they should redouble their efforts to understand the capital markets, and in a world in which clearing is assuming greater importance, those technologists [who] understand clearing will have an edge.

Key Learning Points

- When a firm approaches data, it should have a clear understanding of what questions it wants that data to answer for it. Firms must not only invest in intelligent processing of data but also in intelligent presentation of Big Data so that businesses can better see the value.

- Intelligent software is helping people use data to derive business benefits. For example, there are a number of data visualization tools on the market, and they are becoming increasingly adept at providing a very good quick overview of data. In the highly specialized financial markets, however, technology is insufficient in and of itself. It requires guidance from humans with experience in the subject matter.

- Honing in on certain data may seem like a pragmatic approach but it is not a farsighted one. While firms can be relatively certain what data adds value today, five years in the future, different pieces of a data set could prove invaluable.

BIG DATA, BIG OPPORTUNITIES

CHAPTER 16

Social Media in Trading

Making Sense of It

M any market participants are turning to data for their next source of edge, as we saw in the previous chapter on Big Data. As solutions emerge that help them extract value from massive amounts of data, market participants are able to consider more data sources as inputs to their models. One such source of data that could prove to be extremely valuable for trading and other firms is social media. In this chapter, Joe Gits of Social Market Analytics, a firm that produces trading signals based on social media, discusses what insights social media can offer and how market participants can separate meaningful data from the noise.

With over 500 million tweets per day, everyone, active user or not, knows that social media is where highly relevant private and public conversations are taking place. Social media in itself needs only the briefest introduction: Users post private and public commentary online for the benefit of an audience that includes both "friends" and the wider public. See Figure 16.1.

Monitoring these conversations and the massive quantities of data that they entail in the search for the mention of corporate names has been the key area of activity for many social market entrepreneurs. Proper nouns are easier to pick up in searches, and corporate players often have larger budgets to finance monitoring activity. An increase in social media

153

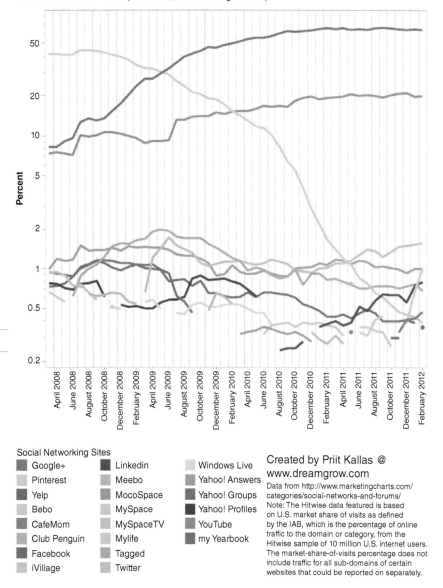

Top 10 Social Networking Sites & Forums 2008–2012
U.S. Market Share of Visits (Priit Kallas, www.dreamgrow.com)

Social Networking Sites

■ Google+	■ Linkedin	▒ Windows Live
▒ Pinterest	■ Meebo	■ Yahoo! Answers
■ Yelp	■ MocoSpace	■ Yahoo! Groups
■ Bebo	▒ MySpace	■ Yahoo! Profiles
■ CafeMom	▒ MySpaceTV	■ YouTube
▒ Club Penguin	■ Mylife	■ my Yearbook
■ Facebook	■ Tagged	
▒ iVillage	■ Twitter	

Created by Priit Kallas @
www.dreamgrow.com
Data from http://www.marketingcharts.com/
categories/social-networks-and-forums/
Note: The Hitwise data featured is based
on U.S. market share of visits as defined
by the IAB, which is the percentage of online
traffic to the domain or category, from the
Hitwise sample of 10 million U.S. internet users.
The market-share-of-visits percentage does not
include traffic for all sub-domains of certain
websites that could be reported on separately.

FIGURE 16.1   Reprinted with permission of www.dreamgrow.com, www.dreamgrow
.com/top-10-social-networking-sites-market-share-of-visits/

mentions can be caused by any number of factors, ranging from a customer service snafu to an employee restructuring, and can impact a company and its share price proportionally. For these reasons and others, savvy corporations have been on the cusp of developments in scrutinizing social media. These companies, in a variety of sectors, have taken proactive steps to monitor social media usage by their employees and stakeholders primarily for the purposes of branding, compliance, competitive intelligence, or investor relations.

Despite the fact that much of social media monitoring is currently done for regulatory purposes, trading firms are keenly aware of the reward—and conversely—risk potential that social media represents. Financial markets' heightened interest lies in the edge of early detection of market-moving posts. Notwithstanding the 500 million daily tweets, only a small percentage of social media activity is relevant for traders. The rest is noise. The challenge for the financial markets lies in culling through a massive number of data points to find tradable information. This interview with Joe Gits, co-founder of Social Market Analytics, focuses on extracting value from social market data and the quantification of social media activity for the purpose of actionable trade signals.

Following are a few statistics from the 2012 Fortune 100 Social Media Statistics Report[*]:

- There are over 10 million social mentions of the Fortune 100 each month.

- Twitter generates the most amount of chatter.

- 87 percent of the Fortune 100 now use social media, with Twitter the most popular.

- Tweet volumes tripled in the last 12 months.

- 75 percent of the Fortune 100 are on Facebook.

- Each corporate YouTube Channel averages 2 million views.

- Fortune 100 companies are creative multiple accounts per platform/per region.

- 50 percent of Fortune 100 companies have a Google+ account.

- 25 percent have a Pinterest account.

---

[*] www.digitalbuzzblog.com/slideshare-fortune-100-social-media-statistics-2012/.

Throughout this book, many of the companies represented by the interviewees are technology innovators in that they have repurposed technology for novel applications to financial services problems. Joe Gits and his company, Social Market Analytics, is yet another example of this phenomenon.

The possibilities that online conversations represent in terms of trade signals are endless and the utilization of them as such will likely develop in waves as the low-hanging fruit is harvested. Entrepreneurs around the world are developing novel ways to gather or generate social media data that provide insights into consumer patterns including traditional consumer products as well as in areas like fossil fuel utilization. Farmers are electronically conversing about the quality of their crops and livestock. Currency traders are commenting on economic releases and their impacts on exchange rates. These conversations often possess actionable intelligence for people with the ability to find and quantify it.

First popular in cash equity and equity derivatives markets, social media signals are gaining traction in the currency, bond, and commodity markets as an increasing number of conversations on important geopolitical and other topics take place. Europe's sovereign debt crisis and the Arab Spring illustrate just a couple of the potentially actionable macroeconomic threads that social media conversations reflect.

Although it takes time to accumulate statistically significant chatter about a company or event, many high-frequency firms look for market segments or equities that exhibit volatility, which in itself takes time to display. In addition, social media data is stream-of-consciousness communication, which means that it is not subject to the sometimes time-consuming verification requirements as news outlets are. As a result, changes in sentiment often become evident prior to the publication of a news story. Thus, this type of information serves as an early warning system for high-frequency trading (HFT) and can also be used by less latency-sensitive trading and investment firms.

Social media activity is also a growing area of relevance in risk management. If there is an unusually heavy amount of chatter on a sector or equity held in a portfolio, risk managers must be alert to the potential need for hedging or liquidating a certain position.

■ Joe Gits, Social Market Analytics

Joe Gits is the co-founder of Social Market Analytics, a firm that parses and quantifies postings on social market media, turning them into actionable trade signals. Social Market Analytics sells its social market signals to market participants. The company does not engage in proprietary trading activities.

Previous to launching his current venture, Joe co-founded Quantitative Analytics, which he sold to Thomson Financial in 2006. He remained with Thomson Financial, where he oversaw the development of quantitative databases and applications and managed a global team of over 150 developers. His team integrated and maintained Thomson Reuters and third-party content with a special emphasis on security masters and corporate actions.

Why should traders pay attention to social media?

Social media is an exponentially growing method of communication. Many of the conversations that take place via social media concern stocks, pricing, and market movements. These conversations also discuss breaking news stories about securities. Properly identifying and quantifying this data give users an information advantage. Social media is the next information input for algorithmic trading. It is becoming an important variable.

Can you provide an overview of some of the types of social media activity that are proving relevant for traders?

Social media data is proving valuable in a number of different areas. Early warnings of mergers and acquisitions (M&A) activity (for example, Bristol-Myers Squibb's acquisition of Inhibitex, Inc. on January 7, 2012) were posted on social media, as were unofficial high-profile earnings announcements like Facebook. Also, conversations on social media have provided early indicators of scandals. From a risk perspective this data is valuable as an early warning system.

Can you give an example of social media providing a valuable trade signal?

One of the best recent examples is Best Buy being purchased by its founder.

In the pre-market of August 6, 2012, Richard Schulze, founder and former chairman of Best Buy Co., Inc. (NYSE: BBY), submitted a written proposal to the Best Buy board of directors to acquire all of the outstanding shares of the company that he did not already own for a price of $24.00 to $26.00 per share in cash. The proposed purchase price was at a premium of 36 percent to 47 percent to Best Buy's closing stock price of $17.64 on August 3, 2012. Schulze was Best Buy's largest shareholder, controlling 20.1 percent of Best Buy shares.

Mr. Schulze's announcement occurred after 8:15 AM Eastern time. Social Market Analytics computes S-Factor™ metrics continuously at 15-minute bucketed intervals intraday and we detected significant chatter about Best Buy. Our S-Factors detected the leading edge of the social media signature of Schulze's announcement during the computation of the 8:30 AM bucket for Best Buy.

Figure 16.2 shows the dramatic change in Best Buy's S-Score™ and S-Volume™ as the event unfolded. At that time, the takeover bid was being widely discussed on social media in a favorable way, which resulted in our algorithm detecting what we call "High Positive" sentiment and an unusual, rapid increase in social media activity for the stock as indicated by S-Volume.

The major financial news services (Bloomberg, Reuters, and *Wall Street Journal*) began publishing headline stories covering this development starting at 8:44 AM, a full 15 minutes after our detection. This event is an excellent example showing that social media activity can be a leading indicator relative to traditional financial news services.

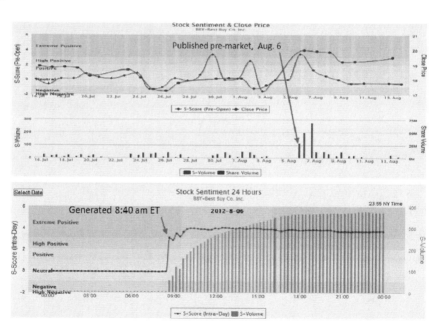

FIGURE 16.2   Reprinted with permission of Social Market Analytics.

In 140 characters, give us a practical example of how you quantify social media posts to create an actionable signal.

Oh, that's funny. Here goes: We calculate the average sentiment of all identified tokens to produce an aggregate of sentiment for the tweet on a scale of −1.0 to 1.0.

Is social media revolutionary to finance?

The novelty with social media is its conversational aspect—the viral, uncontrollable nature of it. And while that presents challenges to special members of our community including regulators, compliance personnel, and even brand managers, for traders, it is business as usual. Markets keep evolving and to stay competitive, good traders adapt to changes in technology, market behavior, [and so forth]. Social media is just one [of the current ones].

Social media is not revolutionary in its content; it is breaking news. And trading is all about processing information and acting upon it faster than anyone else—getting an edge. The challenge for traders with social media is that it is unstructured. Unstructured data is inherently hard to analyze. We turn this unstructured data into quantifiable metrics familiar to traders.

We believe that for professional traders social media data is a required component in factor models. When it comes to qualitative and technical traders, we foresee that they will start charting intra-day sentiments just as they do prices and volume. For retail traders this data will be another piece of information they have on their trading screen.

Have these behavioral changes already started to occur?

Traditional media is ahead of the game in terms of adoption. In fact, virtually every contemporary news show now features a "what's trending in social media" piece.

While these behavioral changes are only starting to occur in capital markets, there is incredible interest in information generated by or from social media. Until now there has really been no way to practically quantify this information and traders need to quantify this data in order to gauge the impact on their models.

Another interesting parallel development is in the field of natural language processing (NLP), which aims to enable computers to derive meaning from human language. Given the diverse postings on social media in terms of language, grammatical quality, [and so forth], advances in NLP could represent a real "edge" in systematic analysis.

Why are you at the forefront of social media and finance?

The belief that social media contains trade signals is obviously not unique to us. What is unique to us is the proprietary software that we have built to systematically compile signals from diverse data points. We are, if you will, at the intersection of social media and trading.

At Social Market Analytics we believe that we are the first to accumulate and parse social media data on a large scale for actionable trade signals. Like other leading firms that regard social media from a compliance perspective, we also view the data from a statistical standpoint. However, our aim is different and so we're looking at different patterns and asking distinctive questions.

We comb through vast amounts of social media data and distill it to create easily interpreted data points for traders. Traders focus on mathematical measurements like standard deviations, volatility, and averages, which feature prominently in our proprietary models. With our data they get a concise, easy-to-digest report of activity and bias in social media. And given our combined experience in the amalgamation of different data sets, we are highly experienced in dealing with Big Data.

How have you addressed the challenges posed by Big Data?

The financial industry has always had to tackle Big Data problems, and so our developers are used to working with large datasets. Two of the biggest technological achievements in the marketplace to date are arguably the readily available open source technologies that permit the quick processing of massive amounts of data coupled with innovations in storage capabilities that have allowed trading firms to warehouse market data. Together they have allowed for incredible advances in trading analytics.

Who else is doing what you are doing?

There are a number of firms that analyze social media data. However, most of these companies focus solely on providing services to corporations, whereas our focus is specifically trading firms. Our management team comes from a trading technology background, so interpreting social media and creating signals for traders is our wheelhouse trade.

How has your technology directly impacted the market?

We have opened the door for members of the trading community to analyze the information coming from social media. Traders are always on the lookout for new information, and we provide a way for traders to use the expansive and growing communication platform that is social media as an input in their trading systems.

Traditional financial data has been analyzed extensively and new sources of edge are at a premium. Simply put, we provide a new set of quantitative data for traders.

Will social media replace important scheduled economic releases?

We feel that eventually there will be broad-based sentiment indicators acting as proxies for scheduled economic data releases. In our view, sentiment data will certainly lead economic data. In a sense, it is an extension of the old trader's maxim: "buy the rumor, sell the fact." Social media is accelerating the time frame at which we receive the same information [included in the releases].

We predict that indicators based on social media will be more sensitive than your traditional economic indicator—in part because they will be more current and they will be comprised of a much broader participant base. One example is if more people are experiencing job losses, a social media broad-based sentiment index would downtick more quickly than a once-a-week update of jobless numbers. So, the added sensitivity could be a positive development in terms of volatility, which traders like.

People are utilizing social media to share running commentaries on their lives. And as I am sure that most people will agree, sometimes those posting commentaries lack a filter. Despite how we may feel about it on a personal note, the lack of filter means traders get access to more data points on social media, which tends to complicate analysis. Are people complaining about their employer or is something larger underway?

Is social media applicable to/suitable for high-frequency trading?

Absolutely. Sentiment can change for many reasons and it can happen very quickly. That being said, a savvy trader will not act on an isolated social media post, and sometimes, social media signals take time to build into something indicative.

Social media posts that hold relevance for the capital markets come in a few flavors. As traders everywhere know, when signals that originate from diverse places line up to support each other, the relevance increases.

Does the time it takes to aggregate social media activity and then distill it to get a trade signal decrease its worth for traders?

No, the time it takes to aggregate the data does not decrease its value. The value is in the distillation of what is happening in social media into quantifiable signals. Although the sentiment can change rapidly, our intra-day calculation engine picks up and publishes the changes in sentiment.

> The value is in the distillation of what is happening in social media into quantifiable signals.

How have algo firms driven your development?

Algo trading has certainly driven my personal and career development as well as the trajectory of Social Market Analytics. My previous firm provided fundamental data and analytics to the capital markets space, and there I learned how quants and algo traders want to see data and the metrics they use to analyze it. At Social Market Analytics, our data was purpose-built to provide those metrics—in a format that algo firms and others can easily integrate into their models. We provide metrics with appropriate volatility and variance numbers so users can measure significance of signals.

While algo firms are important customers of ours, the social media signals that we sell are applicable to a wider range of trading strategies. And while that is a diversification strategy for us, it is also the reality that a variety of investment time frames can capitalize on social media signals.

Can you discuss the regulatory challenges that social media poses for you specifically?

As we discussed, the lion's share of the social media monitoring market segment is focused on meeting corporate compliance needs in terms of social media. For our firm specifically, the fact that we are providing actionable trader signals means that we are subject to oversight. Given the fact that we gather, maintain, and parse databases, recordkeeping is part of our business model. Regulations about the storage and redistribution of social media would have a critical impact on our firm.

In your opinion, what is the next "quantum leap" in trading technology that will revolutionize our industry?

As information flows become near real time, I foresee neural networks becoming more important. Advances in technology, certainly including social media, mean that too much information is coming in too quickly for the human brain to effectively serve as a first filter. We will increasingly rely on machines as preliminary filter to sort out the noise. Then, they can present the summation to decision makers, which can be human or algorithmic. The filter of the social media component is the niche we fill.

How are you implementing IT innovations from the broader industry? Do you actively seek non-financial industry sources?

We built our analytics framework to be industry agnostic, though our specialty is financial markets. Our experience shows us that capital market participants tend to be the most analytical, which makes sense because analytics drive trading decisions and therefore profitability, whereas in other industries it is driven predominantly by product sales. However, we find that other industries are eager learners, adopting from the analytics used in the financial industry.

How do universities or research facilities play a role in your development process?

We are cultivating relationships with universities because of a number of reasons. Social media is such a new space that we need the mindshare provided by academic papers. Moreover, the developers and users of social media in many cases are young people, and we feel that it is essential to maintain a strong link with young minds and how they utilize social media. Students are another source of our competitive edge.

In addition, we have made our data available to a range of university departments. We are working together with academics in behavioral economics, asset pricing, marketing, regression analysis and forecasting, media and communications, and politics. In an appropriate close to our interview, the fact that such a wide range of areas is involved with social media underscores its reach—and thus its appeal to financial markets.

What special technical challenges does social media present?

Social media is unique because of its unstructured nature. With a standard financial dataset one knows roughly how many records should be received and what each record will have in it. The fields are well defined and there is little room for interpretation. In contrast, with social media one has no idea how many records will be sent or what securities will be mentioned in those records. Are the records important, and if so what is the meaning of the record? It is a very interesting problem. The technologies to parse these records are quickly evolving so that adds an interesting dynamic.

Do you have any special lessons for technologists?

We have learned that filtering techniques for identification of indicative information in social media are critically important. We find that the signal-to-noise ratio is about 10 percent. Making sure your filters are current and effective is critically important.

Key Learning Points

- Trading is about processing information and acting upon it faster than anyone else—getting an edge. The challenge for traders with social media is that it is unstructured. Unstructured data is inherently hard to analyze.

- Conversations on social media have provided early indicators of scandals. From a risk perspective, this data is valuable as an early warning system.

- We predict that indicators based on social media will be more sensitive than your traditional economic indicator—in part because they will be more current and they will be comprised of a much broader participant base.

CHAPTER 17

The View from Emerging Markets, China

E merging financial markets are quickly developing into areas of opportunity, both for local companies and global market participants. These
young markets are diverse, characterized by different market structures and
unique regulations. It is ill advised for firms to follow a one-size-fits-all approach when considering participation in such markets.

On the technology side, emerging financial markets are gleaning insight
from established financial markets and opting to self-develop solutions that
fit local needs at the same time. This tendency is both positive and negative.
On the one hand, companies are experimenting with innovative ideas and
are arguably the best at understanding local requirements. On the other
hand, by opting out of global standards like FIX (Financial Information
eXchange), some in emerging markets unwittingly make it harder for them
to compete on a global scale.

Although emerging markets are later entrants to the financial markets,
they do provide valuable lessons in effective utilization of technology to
address business needs. In this chapter, Ming Hua of Southwest Securities
Company provides his insights on the state of the Chinese financial markets,
business concerns, and how Chinese brokerage firms are leading the global
markets in harnessing mobile technology to serve the vast retail-based community and engender customer loyalty.

167

■ Ming Hua, Southwest Securities Company

Ming Hua is currently designate chief technical director in the department of information technologies of Southwest Securities Co., Ltd., located in Chongqing, China. His group is responsible for the firm's IT strategic planning, IT service requests management, and IT system design and development. Prior to this role, from January 2009 to October 2012, he served as chief architect of the Information & Technology Center of China Merchants Securities Co., Ltd. (CMS) in Shenzhen, China. Before joining CMS, he spent more than eight years in the financial services sector and five years in the telecommunication industry in the United States from 1997 to 2008, and successively worked with AT&T Labs, IBM Global Services, UBS Financial Services, and Magnetar Capital. He holds a bachelor's degree in science from Fudan University in Shanghai, China, and a master's degree in electrical engineering from the University of Texas at Dallas in the United States.

How are emerging financial markets like China different from those in established markets in terms of the technology solutions they demand?

Due to strict regulations, incomplete market structures, financial infrastructures that are still in the development process, and limited financial products, Chinese markets are generally retail investor-based so far. This is particularly true for the stock market. For example, by the end of 2011, there were 162 million retail A share equity trading accounts compared with only 0.61 million institutional A share accounts in China, which corresponds to 98.18 percent versus 0.4 percent, respectively.

Most importantly, retail investors hold 26.5 percent of all tradable A shares, compared to 15.6 percent held by institutional investors (the rest are held by various business entities). Furthermore, retail investors contribute more than 85 percent of the daily trading volumes, and most of the 114 Chinese securities firms in China earned more than 40 percent of their total operational income from retail brokerage services.

For the reasons mentioned, systems used to support the retail community have been vital. Currently, backend systems are where [the] bulk of development is taking place. First of all, a highly efficient and extremely stable centralized trading platform is of critical importance for securities firms to compete with each other. In addition, the development and improvement of compliance systems, risk management systems, valuation systems, clearance and settlement systems, enterprise data warehouses, [and so forth], together also consume a big chunk of available budgets.

As financial products and services are limited in China, securities firms have continued to develop systems to differentiate themselves from competitors. One prime example is the importance of mobile services, which is amplified by the vast size of the Chinese markets and number of retail investors. With the advancement of cellular-based infrastructure and mobile technologies, securities firms have popularized mobile investing and supported this with [a] lion's share of development efforts. Securities firms are also actively working on value-add wealth management systems to carry out portfolio analysis, investment consulting, wealth planning, and discretionary management services for customers with different net worth, investment goals, and risk profiles.

Regarding new business opportunities, in pace with the recent relaxation in regulation on the part of China Securities Regulatory Commission (CSRC), we now are focusing more attention on our institutional and high-net-worth customers, which we believe is the new trend in China. We have started the design and development of our quantitative trading platform based on complex event processing (CEP) engine, an over-the-counter (OTC) trading system that supports order matching and market making for equities and derivatives, and a custodian system for prime brokerage services.

Are emerging markets ahead of or behind established markets in terms of technology? Do fewer legacy systems give you the advantage of starting from a clean slate?

Emerging markets are definitely behind in terms of trading technology. In this area, we are learning from established markets. One advantage is that emerging markets have fewer legacy systems in place, which makes it easier to start from scratch. As a new entrant, China is making huge strides in financial market technology within a short time frame. One must remember that Chinese markets have been extant for only 22 years.

> One advantage is that emerging markets have fewer legacy systems in place, which makes it easier to start from scratch. As a new entrant, China is making huge strides in financial market technology within a short time frame.

Emerging markets technologists are at an advantage because we can select from readily available technologies and have many examples of successful—and some not so successful—implementation efforts.

Are global standards like FIX facilitating the integration of emerging markets?

In China, many standard technologies, such as web services, J2EE, and .NET, have been adopted to facilitate systems integration in the financial industry.

Regarding the exchange of securities trading data, instead of using FIX directly, CSRC launched a new protocol called the STEP (Securities Trading Exchange Protocol) as Chinese security industry standard in March 2005. Official reports said that STEP is the localization of FIX4.4 and it will be interoperable with FIX. Up to now, except the applications in level II market data services by Shanghai and Shenzhen Stock Exchanges, STEP has not actually been used in trading by Chinese brokerage firms, and the Chinese futures exchanges also have not adopted STEP in their businesses yet.

In my opinion as a technologist, if we in China would like to establish interconnections between exchanges or brokerage firms, and expand globally, we need to harness international technology standards more openly and actively. The rationale is simply that everyone else uses them and barriers to integration would be significantly lower.

Do technology partnerships constrain emerging market technologists?

Partnerships can be double-sided. They help companies get the systems that they need at reduced time to market. However, the drawback is that the dependency on a provider could become very strong for some financial companies, especially for those that lack internal development strength. In China, companies are extremely cost sensitive, and this focus on costs also promotes dependency because the large hardware / software vendors benefit from economies of scale and can offer lower prices. This cost advantage is coupled with the fact that once interpersonal relationships are established, they tend to remain in place. So, the incentive to "stick" with the same provider is strong. Incidentally, you can see this in action in China, where there are only three major vendors of financial IT systems. The exception to this is at the exchange level, where the government has been very vocal in promoting self-development. It sees the development of proprietary exchange technology as a matter of national interest.

On the technology front, what is the greatest operational challenge in China and other emerging markets?

As they are in other markets, reliability and efficiency are of the utmost importance. However, given the strict investor-protection rules and the government's central aim of maintaining social stability in China, the negative effects of a system going down, which could cause investment losses for clients, would be extremely detrimental to a securities firm's standing. On top of losing face, Chinese regulators impose stiff penalties on companies with significant system failures; they can even lose their licenses on certain business for repeat problems. This not only pertains to execution systems but extends to areas like market data as well.

How do regulations in emerging markets drive technological innovation?

Regulations are important in that they set both standards as well as penalties for non-compliance. In terms of innovation, regulation can sometimes act as a drag since it is always behind the rapidly changing markets by nature. Chinese financial markets are tightly supervised by CSRC with regard to what products and services different types of financial companies can offer, so technological innovations are restricted accordingly.

However, things have started to change in China. We are excited to welcome a new chairman of CSRC, Mr. Guo Shuqing. Since he assumed the office in October 2011, he has taken a series of actions to help liberalize the markets. On May 7, 2012 he kicked off an innovation conference involving all securities firms to discuss how to develop securities' business through innovations, and pushed forward 11 new policies after the conference to promote and support innovation. This is a welcome development; securities firms are now allowed to build up their own OTC businesses, and offer new products and services to establish their core competencies in trading, investment, financing, custody and settlement, and payments functions. Restrictions on investment scope, net capital limits, leverage, [and so forth] have been relaxed as well. In the process of building up new profit centers and establishing a more enduring business model, technological innovation will play a critical role for all securities firms.

What can established financial markets learn from you, the new entrants?

In China, efficient utilization of mobile technology is an important determinant of a brokerage business's success. Because of the sheer numbers and geographic dispersion of Chinese customers, Chinese securities firms are providing their clients most front-end services through mobile devices.

For leading securities firms, over 30 percent of customers use mobile platforms for trading and other investing services already. Among young people, it is probably the most important consideration in attracting and retaining new customers. We compete on things such as providing the fastest and most reliable market data service and order processing through mobile platforms. Mobile usability is something we regularly upgrade.

Additional value-add services, including portfolio-related market news and investment advice, are offered via mobile text messaging. For leading securities firms, each of them usually sends millions of text messages to customers every business day. We also harness satellite communication networks to provide market data and online trading services.

Are emerging markets more likely to give local technology firms an opportunity or are they more likely to deploy big names to benefit from a global name?

The Chinese government generally provides strong support to local Chinese technology companies, and part of that is to promote their competitiveness on a global level. But global giants like IBM and Oracle still have strong footprints in China.

The government can and does provide similar support for the Chinese financial markets. The CSRC works with local vendors closely on the technology side. In fact, some of the exchanges' trading systems are co-developed by the exchanges and local IT system providers.

While mature technologies from the established markets, such as message-oriented-middleware (MOM) products TIBCO or 29West, are available to us, the reality in China is that some large system vendors or financial institutions prefer to develop similar technologies themselves in a variety of situations. That is definitely positive in the sense of lower cost and controlling the key technologies in our own hands, but it could be an obstacle when it comes to system integration and reliability. Too much "own" technology and "own" communication protocols will limit the interoperability within our markets as well as globally.

How are financial technologists in different emerging markets learning from each other?

First of all, Chinese market participants visit other emerging markets and established markets often to exchange ideas, and get hands-on lessons on both business models and technology practice. In the meantime, we also invite financial institutions of other emerging/established markets and leading global IT vendors, who are highly interested in gaining a foothold in China, to visit us and share their insights. Within Asian emerging markets there is probably the most interaction. Chinese regulators and market participants have successfully adopted a lot of what they learned through these mutual communications to build up and further develop financial markets in China.

How do emerging market financial players grow new talent?

Paradoxically, despite the high numbers of technologists that China produces, finding qualified technologists for financial market systems is difficult here as well. The [rarest] talents are those who know how to architect a large-scale high-performance system and build it from scratch, and those [who] understand how to integrate heterogeneous systems.

In order to improve employees' skill sets, IT departments of Chinese financial companies have proactive yearly training plans, including sending people for training courses to acquire both hard skills and soft skills. More and more in-house IT projects in recent years also give Chinese technologists opportunities to enhance their skills through real-life practice.

In addition, Chinese market participants also hire IT experts with hands-on experience from established markets abroad to help them out. Doing so provides them with very valuable know-how to effectively improve the quality of overall system design and development, and build up local IT teams.

What keeps you up at night?

Capacity and disaster recovery [are] always at the top of my list. We have invested a great deal in system stability already but at the expense of some efficiency. However, as traditional "channel" services are shrinking and of high homogeneity, Chinese securities firms have come to a turning point where they have to seek further business development through transformation and innovation, so the chief challenge for me is devising ways to make my company competitive from a technology standpoint.

In order to support the products and services newly permitted by CSRC, and to meet the challenges from foreign big-name players that will emerge as our competition with the further opening up of Chinese financial markets, we will have to overhaul existing systems and introduce plenty of advanced technologies and platforms from established markets. I spend a lot of time considering how best to achieve goals within constraints such as lack of talent, tight budgets, [and so forth].

What would you list as the most important technological achievement within the financial services industry within the last several years? How has it been a game changer?

Cloud computing will likely be very valuable going forward in China, based on the aforementioned concerns of cost and reliability. Clouds offer more scalable and manageable services that can help Chinese market participants expand their IT footprints at reasonable cost.

In your opinion, what is the next "quantum leap" in trading technology that will revolutionize our industry?

Quantum computers would be a huge advance. They could be a million times faster than digital computers based on transistors. But we will have to wait a long time for a practical model in reality. A more realistic expectation is the introduction of a superfast mobile network. Currently the 4G network could reach the speed of about 10 mbps on average, so a multigigabit mobile network could be a quantum leap. A jump in throughput like that would bring revolutionary changes into our daily life, and encourage a lot more customers of securities firms to use services delivered through wireless devices.

Key Learning Points

- In China, efficient utilization of mobile technology is an important determinant of a brokerage business's success. Because of the sheer numbers and geographic dispersion of Chinese customers, Chinese securities firms are providing their clients most front-end services through mobile devices.

- As traditional "channel" services are shrinking and of high homogeneity, Chinese securities firms have come to a turning point where they have to seek further business development through transformation and innovation.

- Securities firms are now allowed to build up their own OTC businesses, and offer new products and services to establish their core competencies in trading, investment, financing, custody and settlement, and payments functions. Restrictions on investment scope, net capital limits, leverage, [and so forth] have been relaxed as well.

CHAPTER 18

Special Focus

The Shortage of IT Talent

In this special section, Daryan Dehghanpisheh of NYSE Technologies discusses a very serious problem facing the industry: How can firms meet the increasing day-to-day demands of their growing technology infrastructures, discover promising applications, and implement new technology in new ways that add value, all without sufficient staff?

177

This book has covered a broad range of major topical issues in financial technology but is far from complete. As such, it presents only a partial picture of the scope of the IT challenges facing the industry. How and how effectively firms approach new technology is only part of the problem. Maintenance of existing systems also places high demands on IT departments. This chapter provides a sobering perspective on how a dearth of qualified IT talent is acting as a brake on IT innovation.

An image problem also contributes to the scarcity of IT talent in our industry. The financial crisis, high-profile incidents, and general economic malaise have negatively impacted people's opinions of the financial industry and, in doing so, made financial services a less-attractive employer in the eyes of many. As has been well documented in the popular media, young people are increasingly choosing professions that are less structured and more social in nature. In the tech area, rapid growth and rewarding compensation packages can be found in Silicon Valley. This combination of factors complicates the job of finding technology talent for financial services.

As this chapter stresses, there is also good news in this situation, including opportunity for gifted technologists who decide to work in the markets.

Smaller, more nimble firms within the industry are regarded as especially attractive employers in part because of their focus on cutting-edge technology.

■ Daryan Dehghanpisheh, NYSE Technologies

Daryan Dehghanpisheh holds a bachelor's degree in computer science from the University of Arizona. Representative of many students with an interest in applied technology, he selected the school because it offered a financial package partly backed by leading technology companies and thus offered a close relationship between technology students and the field. Intel Corporation sponsored his undergraduate research efforts and he began his career with the corporation by working on the Intel Pentium® Microarchitecture project.

Early in Daryan's career he moved to New York City to help the company establish a formidable competitive position within the finance industry. From there, he was promoted to chief of staff and technical advisor to the executive who oversaw Intel's $25B+ Digital Enterprise group. In 2010, he decided to apply his passion for technology and the markets by joining NYSE Euronext's Technology division, NYSE Technologies. There he is responsible for architecting and deploying custom electronic trading solutions for hedge funds, large banks, and other global market players.

Just how difficult is it to find qualified technologists in our industry? With whom are we competing?

Finding great talent is always challenging. However, a number of factors have complicated the talent search in financial services. Recent headline events like Occupy Wall Street, congressional hearings, debates around the merits of high-frequency trading (HFT), and many others have generated negative public sentiment. Reduced pay in the industry has also exacerbated the situation. A further complication is the ongoing use of legacy technology. Legacy technology is not exactly an inspiring attraction when seeking to hire the best talent.

Prior to the financial crisis, it was "cool" to work at a large firm as a programmer and technologist. Since then, public sentiment and attitude toward finance has turned many technologists away from the financial industry. They have instead taken their skills to new "cool" startup social networking companies.

Pay was once a big differentiator in favor of financial services. However, in the tech industry, employees often have the ability to take part in exit events like IPOs, plus benefit from generally more competitive labor and pay from a salary basis. This closes this gap. Geography and quality-of-life issues also impact technologists' employment decisions. When one considers the postal codes that finance is in, in fact it may be even easier to make a "better" living outside of these concentration areas of our industry.

The biggest obstacle to hiring is that the financial industry lags from a technological perspective. When comparing the finance industry to a new startup or even old-guard technology companies, it is the legacy stacks that hobble us most. Across a number of high-profile financial trends, from big data to mobile development, in most cases we are not using the latest technologies and the latest tools, and working with cutting-edge technology motivates driven technologists.

Presently, the utilization of legacy technology in financial services is because of both a lack of capability and a lack of will. Executives still often do not see the value of "rip and replace" from a return on equity (ROE) perspective. Better technology can and does produce better results, but only if you have better talent to design, develop, and manage it.

What's the hardest skill to find?

Given that there is such a wide range of IT projects in our industry, many of which require different specific skills, it is difficult to identify one as the hardest to find. When hiring, I believe that there are two disciplines to evaluate: skills and attributes. It is very easy to hire for any one particular skill. From people who know Open Dremel to a talented network designer, skills can be found, tested, and hired into an organization.

However, attributes and aptitudes are harder to match, both within firms and between prospective hires and potential employers. Finding a programmer who knows C++ but also knows how to integrate into, and possibly lead, a team can be hard. Soft skills and the ability to work effectively as a team member are equally valuable as technical skills because culture clash can be a major barrier to building successful teams.

Currently, the most elusive hires are candidates who are excellent at problem solving and logical argument construction. And if we add creativity into that mix of skills, it complicates the process even more.

The ability to communicate well is essential because technology is already complex, and this complexity is increasing. Few executives in our firms truly understand (or can even keep pace with) the rapid advancements in the tech fields. So, when a technology leader must explain to the business side why the company should rip up outdated solution A for "startup" solution B that may not be as tried and true, he or she must be able to effectively communicate the value to the business. Not only do these investments cost a lot of money but they also may introduce significant operational risk. In a business that is used to evaluating the risk/reward ratio, a technology team needs to be able to make the case as to why a change in technology is so critical and worth the risk—and the expense.

Too often, I see technologists explaining things in a purely technical capacity, but failing to make the case as to why or how something should be done from a business, competitive, and historical perspective. Finding people who are technically excellent but also able to make a logical, compelling case for the reason behind their decisions, is the toughest skill set for the industry to find.

On average, how long does it take to fill a technology role?

Based on subjective personal experience, the entire process can take around two to three months, depending on the specific open position. For lower-level functions like general programmers or system administrators, the process is significantly quicker, as long as the technology and skills in question are common. Specific skills can complicate a job search, especially in the case of candidates that are well equipped to deal with newer technology trends, as in the case of Big Data. Often, when filling those positions managers must re-evaluate their screening criteria, and compromise on employees with basic skill sets and fill in blanks with on-the-job training.

Though it is ill advised to hire technologists solely based on soft skills, oftentimes, technology managers do not place enough emphasis on the interpersonal skills of their potential technology hires. Finding the right personality is one factor that can add significant time to a typical hiring process.

How does the coursework (languages, etc.) being taught in today's technology schools impact the financial industry moving forward?

Many schools are offering advanced courses and classes that teach skills, languages, paradigms, and constructs that our industry cannot adopt now and may not be able to in the medium term. The industry is not ready to be able to effectively use the skills that new graduates have. They are thus, in a sense, wasting potential.

Big Data is where I see this as most acute. Universities are fielding candidates that know how to operate in the new world of Big Data languages and systems, but the industry of finance is far behind being able to utilize these tools to add value.

The industry is not ready to be able to effectively use the skills that new graduates have. They are thus, in a sense, wasting potential.

Big Data is where I see this as most acute.

Heterogeneous computing technologies, which are being explored and taught in universities, are going to be the next big thing for us to grapple with as an industry. The complex types of cores including central processing unit (CPU), graphical processing unit (GPU), and other forms of hardware acceleration will allow for a whole new breed of applications and usage models in our industry and others. We see this today in mobile, it will happen in servers soon enough. Knowing how to harness all this technology will be critical. In addition to developing for this new model, the knowledge of how to evaluate and build reliable quality assurance (QA) and test models will need to change as well.

Finally, the mobile phenomenon at the moment is making coding to actual instruction sets harder. There is value in knowing how to "write to the metal." But, most of the innovation and momentum in coding right now are in areas where there is more abstraction between the hardware and development environment. Fewer and fewer people know how to build a great compiler. Which means there are fewer people who can develop IT tools, for example. Knowing instruction sets for the type of problems the industry is working on now is critical.

How is the current regulatory climate impacting technology hiring?

Regulation drives so much of our decision making, and the financial technology industry is no different. If regulations require firms to store hundreds of times more data and also make that data more transparent, that changes the skill set in demand. Until governments and policy makers decide what they want to do, and how they want us to do it, it will make hiring decisions harder and slower.

Additionally, government needs to hire its own set of technologists that can compete with us. Unfortunately, the search for talent does not seem like a priority for some regulatory agencies. The focus lies in budgets and congressional money allocation. In areas of national security, governments hire the best coders they can find, as do Apple, Facebook, and others. However, in the market regulation areas we seem to "settle" for something less than that. The recent decision by the SEC to use a market participant's technology for monitoring of the equities markets highlights this well.

How does the financial services culture affect applicants?

The irony of our industry is that we prioritize risk management and yet, we seem to be risk adverse in the case of technology. It is difficult to tell someone who is interested in coming to work at a large financial firm that that firm is a "leading technology" company when it utilizes database technology that is 10 years old, storage architecture that is decades old, and operating procedures that date back well into the last century.

A true technologist wants to be innovative and take risks, but the finance industry has yet to reconcile with its modernity. Even some governmental agencies declare the BlackBerry device to be insufficient. Yet, it is still the primary tool for e-mail within our industry and not simply because of the keyboard. Therefore, it is anachronistic to show up for a recruiting meeting on a college campus and be using technology of yesterday when you are trying to hire the talent of tomorrow. Our industry suffers from this disease far too often.

What advantages can the financial industry offer to technologists?

Despite the challenges I have described, this industry still attracts very talented, competitive people who are driven and who will drive their peers in a similar manner. Being surrounded by people who are as smart as, or smarter than, you, is what drives many. On the compensation front, the industry still pays generally well compared to technology roles in other industries outside of the "pure tech" space. The discrete nature of gain/loss in the financial industry is something that many people will always find attractive.

Additionally, when a profit-focused financial firm does decide to unleash its technological potential there is great opportunity for technologists. Once it decides to, the financial industry can invest in some really cutting-edge, innovative ways to utilize technology. Unfortunately, the complicating factor is that not enough of the industry is willing to do this yet. But, that will change as the demographics of the leadership changes. When the next generation of generally more technologically-savvy "new hires" enters the C-level of financial firms then our industry will find parity with other more technology-oriented companies like those in Silicon Valley.

Are there types of market participants that are more attractive to technologists?

Oftentimes, smaller, private firms that specialize in a range of technology and algorithm-based strategies are a better fit for the true technologist. Newer companies that have less legacy thinking, not necessarily legacy systems, are the best places to go. Young firms that specialize in latency arbitrage are great for people who want to write to the particular instruction set. Big macro funds that rely on data-mining skills will be more interesting to data scientists and Big Data programmers.

From a hiring perspective, the firms that are experiencing the biggest challenges are the big bulge bracket firms. There is just too little innovation, and too many politics for the best technologists to thrive. The older a firm, the harder it is for [it] to get competitive in technology elements, generally speaking. While they may have deep pockets to lure talent, they may not be able to deliver the leadership fortitude to invent and innovate. I think the jury is out on that.

Are software or hardware skills at a premium?

Marc Andreessen famously stated, "Software is eating the world." I think this is true—and will be into perpetuity. My advice to any current technologist is to always do what you love. That may be hardware or it may be software, or it may be both. From a hirer's perspective, the industry currently needs more capabilities in software and systems than in hardware development. Software actually makes hardware development easier. For example, building a VLSI CMOS solution gets easier every year as Moore's Law and computing performance allows software to "get smarter" at helping design hardware. It is a virtuous self-feeding cycle, still.

What advice do you have for technologists looking for jobs in our industry?

First off, determine if you and your firm are a good match and discover whether it values technology as highly as you do. If not, continue your search. Understand if the top leadership of the company truly understands technology. Do the CEO and her or his deputies understand that technology underpins everything that happens in the markets? Do they have the policies and culture in place that reflects that? If they do not, you will likely become quickly frustrated, bored, and disappointed, and may quickly decide to switch employers, which results in both new hires and employers wasting resources.

The world's wealth has been virtualized—bits and bytes, not dollars and pounds. Too often the leadership of firms do not understand this and do not build in the institutional attitudes and processes to be truly innovative technology firms. Find out if innovation is truly at the core of the firm, or is it just something on the website and in corporate messaging? If technology is not a core principle, one can make the case that the firm, by extension, fails to understand the technology underpins the markets today, and that its importance will only grow in the future. Ultimately, a firm that fails to "get IT" will deliver software and/or products that are inferior. Further, flawed technology in fast-paced financial markets is an extremely serious concern, as it has the potential to rapidly destabilize markets (e.g., the case of Knight Capital and its flawed algorithms).

When a firm has its R&D elements in the same silo as Core IT, it may be a signal that innovation is not a part of the culture. This is because the culture of Core IT and R&D are vastly different. Core IT needs to be risk adverse and "keep the business running." R&D must be able to take risks and react. Having these two under the same control means that resource discussions may be tense, internal issues may more often win out over external innovation, and product enhancement may lag crisis management. In the technology sector, these two areas are separate and the financial industry could easily adopt the standard best practice.

How would you advise those trying to recruit new technology hires?

Be up front with candidates about what you can and what you cannot take on from a technological risk perspective. Truly innovative, creative people will become frustrated if they feel you have sold them a bill of goods. Hire for culture fit first; technical abilities second; and future potential third. Candidates will respond well to a clearly communicated technology philosophy. Why does your firm believe in technology? Why does your firm believe in innovation? Why does your firm have a competitive technological edge? And, most importantly, why is working at your place great? Finally, among today's more socially conscious hires, why will coming to work with and for you matter?

 ## Key Learning Points

- The biggest obstacle to hiring is that the financial industry lags from a technological perspective. Across a number of high-profile financial trends from Big Data to mobile development, in most cases we are not using the latest technologies and the latest tools, and working with cutting-edge technology motivates driven technologists.

- Oftentimes, smaller, private firms that specialize in a range of technology and algorithm-based strategies work best for the true technologist. Newer companies that have less legacy thinking, not necessarily legacy systems, are the best places to go.

- In a business that is used to evaluating the risk/reward ratio, a technology team needs to be able to make the case as to why a change in technology is so critical and worth the risk—and the expense.

A Call for Continued Education

This book has provided a concise overview of leaders' perspectives on major issues in technology in the financial and commodity markets. Its goal has been to introduce key trends as well as specific technologies that are helping firms address current business challenges, as well as those that are yet to come. In these markets, as in most other industries, technology becomes valuable in context, when applied to business issues.

In their interviews, the leaders took care to make technology accessible, and in doing so bolstered this book's thesis that they excel at both explaining technology to a wider audience and communicating its value to the business of markets.

Technology occupies a central role in today's markets and its importance will continue to grow. As it does, it is essential for the business side to achieve, at the minimum, a topical understanding of major themes in technology in our industry. For a cross-section of readers, by better understanding technology issues, like those profiled in this book, we can build a more productive partnership between IT and business. On the flip side, as many insightful leaders highlighted, work to deepen technologists' understanding of financial and commodity markets also would be a welcome and highly valuable exercise. Effective communication between the business and

IT sides will not only help improve the effectiveness of such projects, but also has the power to make the individual technologists who take the time to learn indispensable.

It is my hope that readers can use this collection of interviews as both a reference book and also as an invitation to delve deeper into specific topics as warranted by their business needs.

In closing, we return to the theme of the visionary. The technology leaders whose interviews appear in this book have, in the past, helped their companies harness technology to enhance their businesses. Not content to rest on their laurels, they have their eyes firmly focused on their visions of the future. They are actively engaged in addressing the challenge of how new technology can drive further improvements, and as such, they serve as a model for us all.

INDEX

INDEX

Printed and bound by CPI Group (UK) Ltd, Croydon, CR0 4YY